MULTICULTURAL BIOGRAPHIES COLLECTION

AFRICAN AMERICAN
BIOGRAPHIES

GLOBE FEARON
EDUCATIONAL PUBLISHER

PARAMUS, NEW JERSEY

Paramount Publishing

Senior Editor: Barbara Levadi
Project Editor: Lynn W. Kloss
Editorial Assistant: Roger Weisman
Writers: Margarete Pruce, Brenda Lane Richardson,
    Frances E. Ruffin, Sandra Widener
Production Manager: Penny Gibson
Art Director: Nancy Sharkey
Production Editor: Nicole Cypher
Marketing Manager: Sandra Hutchison
Interior Electronic Design: Joan Jacobus
Photo Research: Jenifer Hixson
Electronic Page Production: Eric Dawson
Cover and Interior Design: B B & K Design, Inc.
Cover Illustration: Jane Sterrett

Printed in the United States of America.   3 4 5 6 7 8 9 10 99 98

ISBN: 0-835-90838-0

GLOBE FEARON
EDUCATIONAL PUBLISHER
PARAMUS, NEW JERSEY

Paramount Publishing

C O N T E N T S

DEAR STUDENT

You have probably read many biographies since you have been in school. Because no biography can describe everything about a person, a biographer usually writes with a focus, or a theme of the subject's life, in mind. A collection of biographies also has a focus, so that if you wanted to learn, for example, about sports figures or famous scientists, you could quickly find a book that tells about people in these fields.

The biographies presented in this book introduce you to 21 people whose cultural background is African American. The book explores their heritages, and how these heritages influenced their lives. It also reveals how these people became successful in their careers.

The book is divided into four units. Each unit features the life stories of several people whose careers are related to subjects you study in school. The map of the United States on page 1 shows you the locations of the towns and cities in the United States that are mentioned in the biographies.

In addition, a directory of Career Resources and a Bibliography are located at the back of the book. These resources suggest books, magazines, and agencies that can tell you more about the people and careers discussed.

As you read, think about the variety of African American cultural traditions. Notice, too, that even though people have different traditions, all cultures have similarities. By recognizing our similarities and respecting our differences, we can come to know and understand one another.

A C K N O W L E D G M E N T S

p. 4: (top) © Frederick Viebahn; **p. 4:** (bottom) UPI/Bettmann; **p. 5:** (top right) © Kate Kunz, Courtesy of Knopf; **p. 5:** (top left) Jack Manning, NYT Pictures; **p. 5:** (bottom right) UPI/Bettmann; **p. 5:** (bottom left) Courtesy of MacNeil/Lehrer; **p. 6:** Timothy Wright, NYT Pictures; **p. 7:** © Frederick Viebahn; **p. 15:** Archive Photos; **p. 16:** UPI/Bettmann; **p. 24:** AP/Wide World Photos; **p. 25:** © Kate Kunz, Courtesy of Knopf; **p. 33:** Jack Manning, NYT Pictures; **p. 34:** Doug Wilson, NYT Pictures; **p. 42:** © William B. Carter, Courtesy of the Yale Repertory Theater; **p. 43:** UPI/Bettmann; **p. 51:** Courtesy of MacNeil/Lehrer; **p. 52:** Courtesy of MacNeil/Lehrer; **p. 68:** (top) AP/Wide World Photos; **p. 68:** (bottom): UPI/Bettmann; **p. 69:** (top) AP/Wide World Photos; **p. 69:** (middle) © Ari Mintz/New York Newsday; **p. 69:** (bottom left) © Salazar/RETNA Pictures; **p. 69:** (bottom right) AP/Wide World; **p. 70:** Reuters/Bettmann; **p. 71:** AP/Wide World Photos; **p. 79:** UPI/Bettmann; **p. 80:** UPI/Bettmann; **p. 88:** National Museum of American Art, Washington, D.C./Art Resource, NY; **p. 89:** AP/Wide World Photos; **p. 97:** © Ari Mintz/New York Newsday; **p. 98:** © Ari Mintz/New York Newsday; **p. 106:** (left) © Salazar/RETNA Pictures; **p. 106:** (right) AP/Wide World; **p. 107:** (left) AP/Wide World; **p. 107:** (right) AP/Wide World; **p. 124:** (top) © 1994 by Marty Katz; **p. 124:** (bottom) NASA; **p. 125:** (top) Courtesy of California State University; **p. 125:** (middle) Jim Wilson/NYT Pictures; **p. 125:** (bottom) © Nubar Alexanian; **p. 126:** © 1994 by Marty Katz; **p. 127:** © 1994 by Marty Katz; **p. 136:** UPI/ Bettman; **p. 137:** NASA; **p. 145:** Courtesy of California State University; **p. 146:** Courtesy of California State University; **p. 154:** Jim Wilson/NYT Pictures; **p. 155:** Jim Wilson/NYT Pictures; **p. 163:** © Nubar Alexanian; **p. 164:** © Nubar Alexanian; **p. 180:** (bottom) Courtesy of Johnnetta Cole; **p. 180:** (top) Reuters/Bettmann; **p. 181:** (top) Jim Johnson Photography, Courtesy of The NAACP; **p. 181:** (middle) Courtesy of Johnson Publishing Company; **p. 181:** (bottom) © Katherine Lambert/The Children's Defense Fund; **p. 182:** © Damian Strohmeyer, Allsport; **p. 183:** Reuters/Bettmann; **p. 191:** AP/Wide World Photos; **p. 192:** Courtesy of Johnnetta Cole; **p. 199:** Jim Johnson Photography, Courtesy of The NAACP; **p. 200:** Jim Johnson Photography, Courtesy of The NAACP; **p. 207:** Courtesy of Johnson Publishing Company; **p. 208:** Courtesy of Johnson Publishing Company; **p. 217:** © Rick Reinhard/The Children's Defense Fund; **p. 218:** © Katherine Lambert/The Children's Defense Fund.

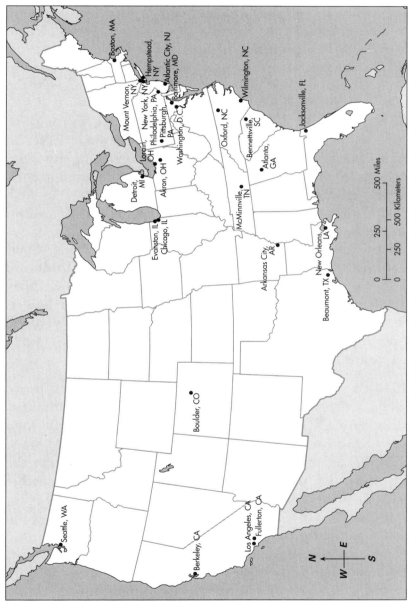

This map shows the locations of cities in the United States that are mentioned in this book.

INTRODUCTION

A biography is a portrait of a person that is presented in words rather than pictures. Details about historical events, personal tragedies and successes, family traits and cultural traditions, and individual talents are often included to help the reader "get to know" the subject.

No biography can tell everything about a person. To try to tell everything would mean that a biographer would write either an enormous book with a great deal of detail about unimportant events, or a book that covers every event, even important ones, very quickly. Biographers, then, must choose the areas they wish to explore so that they will help the reader understand at least part of a person's life fully.

This book introduces you to 21 African Americans. Their biographies focus on three areas of their lives: childhood experiences, cultural heritage, and career goals. Although they are all African American, each person's life story is unique. As you read, you will notice similarities among them, but you will also find that each has his or her own definition of success and of what it means to be an African American.

Childhood experiences often influence the type of individual a person becomes. Particularly exciting or unhappy times can have a major impact. For example, nine-year-old John Johnson had to run for his life during Arkansas City's great flood of 1927. When the water receded, Johnson noticed that the wealthy were able to pull their homes and lives back together faster than poor people like himself. From that time on, Johnson's goal was to build a secure, comfortable life. Today, John Johnson is one of the richest men in the United States.

Writer Carl Rowan tells us about a teacher who influenced his childhood. It was she who told him, "If you don't read, you can't write, and if you can't write, you can stop dreaming."

Some of the people you will read about do not discuss much about their childhood experiences. For them, achievements later in life are more important.

Cultural heritage includes language, religion, and family structure. It is expressed through people's customs, food, clothing, and behavior. Culture is also expressed through art, music, and writing. The lives of some of the African Americans in this book have been shaped by their heritage. For example, artist Jacob Lawrence spent his teenage years in New York City's Harlem, which was the most important cultural center for African Americans at that time.

For others, culture did not become important until adulthood. College president Johnnetta Cole began to explore her African American heritage during a college course.

Career goals reveal a great deal about a person. Some of these biographies tell of commitments to career goals at a very young age. Dancer Judith Jamison, for example, began her training at the age of six.

Other African Americans presented here changed their career goals after they became adults. Poet Rita Dove was planning to be a lawyer when she began her studies at Miami University, and fiction writer Toni Morrison had wanted to be a dancer.

Still others are remarkable because of the variety of their talents or accomplishments. Charles Johnson is a novelist, short-story writer, essayist, and writer of screenplays. He has also been a cartoonist and a philosopher. Like many of this book's subjects, television journalist Charlayne Hunter-Gault and Robert Moses, founder of the Algebra Project, were also active in the Civil Rights Movement.

Many subjects have received awards and honors for their work. Julius Erving, for example, is in the National Basketball Association Hall of Fame. Other people, such as Mae Jemison, who was the first African American astronaut, represent "firsts" in their fields.

Biographies tell a person's life story, but they can also help the reader learn more about himself or herself. As you read, think about these questions: What do you admire about these people? With which points of view do you agree or disagree? Which people and careers do you want to learn more about? In short, what do your reactions to these biographies tell you about yourself?

AFRICAN AMERICANS IN LITERATURE AND COMMUNICATIONS

How do you express yourself? Do you paint, sing, or dance? Perhaps, like the six African Americans in this unit, you use writing to explain your world. As you read, think about how the people in this unit have expressed their thoughts and their heritage in writing.

Rita Dove, Poet Laureate of the United States, says that writing can open people's eyes. "I think people should be shaken up a bit when they walk through life. They should stop for a moment and really look at ordinary things and catch their breath."

Newspaper columnist **Carl Rowan** found that writing can have a powerful effect. His series on discrimination "set in motion a string of events that would change my life forever."

Writer **Toni Morrison** believes that fiction can help African Americans make their voices heard. She explains, "Our silence has been long and deep. We have always been spoken for. Or we have been spoken to."

Fiction writer **Charles Johnson** thinks that all creative work should try to make sense out of the world. "If a story isn't doing that," he says, "then I don't know what it's doing."

Playwright **August Wilson** thinks that drama can help all people understand African American culture. "Black Americans," Wilson says, "have the most dramatic story of all mankind to tell."

Charlayne Hunter-Gault wanted to be a journalist from an early age. "No one ever told me not to dream," she says, "and when the time came to act on that dream, I would not let anything stand in the way of fulfilling it."

As you read this unit, think about how writing has helped each person understand the world and his or her place in it.

RITA DOVE

Poet laureate Rita Dove hopes to use her office to help the American people find the joy that she found in poetry. Dove is only the second woman, and the first African American, to be named poet laureate.

This nutmeg stick of a boy in loose trousers!
Secrets like birdsong in the air.
His pale eyes bright as salt.

Images from music videos? They could be, but they're not. They're lines from the poetry of Rita Dove, a most unusual poet. Like the makers of music videos, she uses quick, powerful images. Her work is rich and accessible.[1] That's the way she wants it. "I think so many of our young people feel that poetry is something they're going to be tested on," she says. She sees it instead as a connection between people. "Poetry is one person talking, whispering to another."

She now has her chance to make poetry as popular as music videos. In 1993, Rita Dove became the youngest person, the second woman, and the first African American to be named Poet Laureate[2] of the United States. The poet laureate helps select poetry books for the Library of Congress in Washington, D.C., and often invites other poets to read their work at the library. Dove sees the job as her chance to bring poetry, and poets, to the attention of Americans. "If only the sun-drenched celebrities are being noticed and worshipped," she says, "then our children are going to have a rough time seeing value in the shadows, where the thinkers, probers, and scientists are who are keeping society together."

Dove says that she was a shy child who preferred the magical life she found in books to the real world. Born in 1952, in Akron, Ohio, she has one older brother and two younger sisters. Her father, who worked for Goodyear Tire and Rubber, was the first African American chemist in the rubber industry. Her mother "always told us stories and encouraged us to do well," Dove says. "I grew up with all sorts of relatives telling stories all the time, so a story well-told is something I learned to appreciate early in life."

1. **accessible** (ahk-SEHS-uh-buhl) *adj.* easy to understand
2. **laureate** (LAWR-ee-iht) *n.* a person who is honored for achievement

When she learned to read, Dove found more stories in books. "From the time I began to read, as a child, I loved to feel their heft[3] in my hand, the warm spot caused by their intimate[4] weight on my lap; I loved the crisp whisper of a page turning, the musky odor of old paper and the sharp inky whiff of new pages. Leather bindings sent me into ecstasy.[5] I even loved to gaze at a closed book and daydream about the possibilities inside." In part, reading was an escape for Dove. "I was painfully shy and awkward," she writes. "The place where I felt most alive was between the pages of a book."

Dove began writing when she was a child. Her first work was "The Rabbit with a Droopy Ear." "It was about a rabbit who needed to get his ear straightened out in time for Easter. He hangs upside down from a tree to do it," Dove says. "I wrote stories often, but to me, writing was play. It was something you did to entertain yourself, like reading."

During the summer, she and her brother were not allowed to watch television. Instead, they read and wrote their own science fiction stories. "During the long, hot summers, my biggest pleasure was to browse[6] along the bookshelf for books that I hadn't read yet. I read many Shakespeare plays, sitting frozen in one postion on the couch for hours. My legs would crumple when I stood up." Over the years, Dove read hundreds of authors, including the work of Langston Hughes. (See **Did You Know?** on page 11 for information on Hughes.)

Dove remembers the thrill she felt when she read her first poem. It seemed like the words floated free on the page. Dove thinks that poetry should be read with that sense of discovery. "I think that when a poem moves you, it moves you in a way that leaves you speechless," she says.

When she was in high school, a teacher brought her to a book-signing of the author John Ciardi (chee-AHR-dee). "Until

---

3. **heft** (HEHFT) *n.* heaviness; weight
4. **intimate** (IHN-tuh-muht) *adj.* familiar; well-acquainted
5. **escstasy** (EHK-stuh-see) *n.* great delight
6. **browse** (BROWZ) *v.* to look casually, reading here and there

then, I didn't think of writing as anything you could do to live. I had never met anyone who did it, so it was the first time I saw real authors and had the inkling[7] that writing was a possible career."

This love of books and learning brought Dove to high school graduation with honors. She was named a 1970 Presidential Scholar—one of the top U.S. graduates that year. The next year, she went to Miami University in Oxford, Ohio. She was going to become a laywer, she thought, "because that was what upwardly mobile,[8] young black kids were supposed to do." When she realized that she was arranging her life around creative writing classes, and that she hated law classes, Dove changed directions. She decided to become a writer.

Her father, she remembers, "put down his newspaper and said, 'Well, I don't understand poetry, so I hope you won't be upset if I don't read it.' To me, that was all the encouragement I needed." After graduating with honors from Miami, she was a Fulbright fellow in Germany for a year. In 1977, she earned her master's degree in creative writing at the University of Iowa. Since then, teaching jobs, awards, and grants for her poetry have supported her. She is also currently a professor of English at the University of Virginia.

In 1980, Dove's first book of poetry, *The Yellow House on the Corner*, was published. It is a journey through six years of Dove's life, beginning with college. "I remember it was a shock to see my first book, and I was afraid to open it for hours. Yet, I still like the book very much—its innocence. It's a young book, full of things that I would never put in a book now, but I wouldn't go back and change anything either."

In that book, she writes about the places she has visited, but she also writes about everyday life. Here is her description of the triumph a student feels when she finally understands something. "I solve a theorem and the house expands: the windows jerk free to hover near the ceiling, the ceiling floats away with a sigh."

---

7. **inkling** (IHNK-lihng) *n.* hint; clue
8. **mobile** (MOH-buhl) *adj.* able to move or advance in social status

Rita Dove wants people to take a closer look at the world that surrounds them. For example, she paints her nails with polka dots. "I like the idea that it makes people startle a little bit and think that maybe not everything is just what meets the eye. I think people should be shaken up a bit when they walk through life. They should stop for a moment and really look at ordinary things and catch their breath."

Dove published *Museum* in 1983. It is a look back at her year in Germany as a Fulbright scholar. The German view of life was completely different from that of Americans, Dove found. "Point of view is everything," she says. The shock of realizing that everyone defines truth differently has made her honest in her own writing. "It's just a duty to write honestly about any situation or character," she says.

Finding the truth behind her grandparents' life story was the reason Dove wrote *Thomas and Beulah*. Some poems are written from her grandfather's point of view, and others from her grandmother's. The poems are full of startling images and memorable language. One character has "gold hawk eyes." Another will "ride joy until it cracks like an egg." Dove says that "working on it was a joy because I felt that I was in the middle of my grandparents' world." *Thomas and Beulah* won the Pulitzer Prize for poetry in 1987, when Dove was 35. She was only the second African American to win this award. Dove appreciates the award for its message to young African Americans. "When I was growing up it would have meant a lot to me to know that a black person had been recognized for his or her writing."

Dove has published several more books of poetry since then, as well as a novel. She and her husband, Fred Viebahn, a novelist from Germany, live in Virginia with their daughter, Aviva. Her daughter, Dove says, has been responsible for many of her recent poems. "She has made me feel more vulnerable,[9] reminding me of youthful experiences through her interests."

Dove has ambitious plans for using the position of poet laureate. But her most important plan is to help people—young

---

9. **vulnerable** (VUL-nuhr-uh-buhl) *adj.* open to damage

people in particular—discover the sense of joy and wonder she found in poems.

Despite the demands of being poet laureate and teaching, Dove always makes time to write. "I don't think I'm any good to my students if I'm not writing, first of all," she says. The reward of that writing is when the poem comes to life and reaches someone else. "There's no greater joy than to have someone else say, 'I know what you mean.' That's real corny, but it's what literature does for all of us, the reader as well as the writer." To touch another person through poetry, Dove says, is "an immensely exciting thing. And that's what I work for."

Did You Know? Like the work of Rita Dove, Langston Hughes's poetry reflects on the African American experience. Hughes is ranked among the major U.S. writers of the 20th century. His poetry, including the books of verse The Dream Keeper *and* Shakespeare in Harlem, *have been translated into many languages. Several were set to music. Born in Joplin, Missouri, in 1902, he began winning poetry competitions while still an undergraduate at Lincoln University in Pennsylvania. In 1935, he was awarded a Guggenheim Fellowship, and in 1960, Hughes was awarded the highly prized Spingarn Medal for his work. He died in 1967.*

AFTER YOU READ

EXPLORING YOUR RESPONSES

1. Dove's position as poet laureate allows her to call attention to poetry. What subject would you like to bring to the attention of more Americans? Explain your answer.

2. Dove was shy and spent her time reading for entertainment. Tell about a book you have enjoyed.

3. Dove read hundreds of books, which helped prepare her for writing poetry. How can reading help a person prepare for a career?

4. Dove's parents did not allow her to watch a lot of television. Do you think children's TV viewing should be restricted? Explain.

5. Dove planned to become a lawyer because of peer pressure. How might peer pressure influence a person's career choice?

UNDERSTANDING WORDS IN CONTEXT

Read the following sentences from the biography. Think about what each underlined word means. In your notebook, write what the word means as it is used in the sentence.

1. Like the makers of music videos, she uses quick, powerful images. Her work is rich and underlined accessible.

2. " 'During the long, hot summers, my biggest pleasure was to browse along the bookshelf for books that I hadn't read yet.' "

3. "I had never met anyone who did it, so it was the first time I saw real authors and had the inkling that writing was a possible career."

4. She was going to become a laywer, she thought, "because that was what upwardly mobile, young black kids were supposed to do."

5. "She has made me feel more <u>vulnerable</u>, reminding me of youthful experiences through her interests."

RECALLING DETAILS

1. What does Dove believe most Americans think about poetry?
2. What was Dove's favorite pastime as a child?
3. How did Dove realize she wanted to be a writer?
4. Name some subjects Dove explores in her poetry.
5. What are some of Dove's accomplishments as a poet?

UNDERSTANDING INFERENCES

In your notebook, write two or three sentences from the biography that support each of the following inferences.

1. Dove wants people to know that poetry is for everyone.
2. Dove helps promote the work of other poets.
3. As a child, Dove did not realize that poetry could be a profession.
4. Dove's heritage influences her work.
5. Dove's daughter has influenced her work.

INTERPRETING WHAT YOU HAVE READ

1. Why do you think it is important to appreciate everyday experiences?
2. How does reading help a person learn?
3. How do you think a poet laureate could help make poetry more popular?
4. Besides finding out the truth about her grandparents, why do you think Dove chose to write about them?
5. Why does Dove think it is important for her students that she keep writing?

ANALYZING QUOTATIONS

Read the following quotation from the biography and answer the questions below.

> *"I think people should be shaken up a bit when they walk through life. They should stop for a moment and really look at ordinary things and catch their breath."*

1. What would it mean to "shake someone up"?

2. Why might Dove want people to look at ordinary things?

3. Think about a book you have read or a song you have heard. What ordinary subject did the author treat in a new and memorable way?

THINKING CRITICALLY

1. How are music videos and poetry similar? How are they different?

2. How do you think being the "youngest" or the "first" in a field might affect a person's work?

3. How do you think watching television influences a person's life?

4. Do you agree or disagree that having poetry on television and radio might help students appreciate it? Why?

5. Dove says she writes so people will say "I know what you mean." What else do you think poetry can do?

CARL ROWAN

Carl Rowan speaks with President Lyndon Johnson in Washington, DC, after his appointment as head of the United States Information Agency. Rowan later resigned from this post to resume his distinguished career in journalism.

It is a dark night in McMinnville, Tennessee, in 1933. Eight-year-old Carl Rowan is asleep on a thin pallet[1] on the floor alongside his brother Charles, his sister Ella, and two cousins. Suddenly, piercing screams wake everyone in the old frame house. Carl's father, Tom Rowan, who is carrying a kerosene lamp for light, runs into the room to comfort his daughter Ella, who has been bitten by a rat. The memory of that night has stayed with Carl Rowan for many years, long after he made his name as one of this country's leading journalists.

Rowan grew up during the Great Depression, in McMinnville, a small lumber mill town. During the Depression, there were few jobs for African American men, and many hungry children. Whenever he could, Tom Rowan stacked lumber for 25¢ an hour. Johnnie Rowan, Carl's mother, taught him how to find watercress and other wild plants that could be added to the family dinner. (See **Did You Know?** on page 29 for more information about the Great Depression.)

Although Carl was valedictorian of his high school class, there was no money for college. One hot July morning, he packed his clothes in a cardboard box and left his parents a note: "I've gone to Nashville for college." His grandparents lived in that city, and he planned to stay with them and study journalism at Fisk University, a historically black college. He had played football in high school, so he hoped to win a football scholarship there.

Pocketing 77¢ and wearing his best clothes, Rowan walked to a local trucking company. He approached a driver and said, "I need a ride to Nashville real bad." He got his ride.

---

1. **pallet** (PAH-liht) *n.* a small bed or pad filled with straw

After being turned down for a football scholarship at Fisk, he picked up his cardboard box of clothing and walked more than a mile to his grandparents' home. Rowan's grandfather, who worked at a hospital, helped Carl find a job there. Carl mopped floors, delivered food to patients, and earned $30 a month. By the end of the summer, Rowan had enrolled in Tennessee State University, another historically black college.

During his third year at Tennessee State, Rowan was selected to take a written exam that would allow him to enter a Navy officer's training program. Rowan became one of the first 15 African Americans in the history of the United States to train to become a commissioned officer.

In 1943, the United States was fighting World War II in Europe and in the Pacific. Carl was assigned to sea duty, and served as a deputy commander of communications aboard the USS *Chemung*. Some Navy officers worried about whether white Southerners would take orders from a young African American officer. Rowan's commander replied, "I'm a Navy man, and we're in war. To me, it's that stripe that counts."

Rowan took this vote of confidence to heart. "When you are plucked out of a totally Jim Crow environment at age 17 and [are] thrown into a totally white environment where more is at stake than your personal life, you mature rapidly." (See **Did You Know?** on page 20 for more information about Jim Crow laws.)

Three years later, the war was over and Rowan was discharged from the Navy. While waiting to take a train home to McMinnville, he settled down with copies of the *Norfolk Journal and Guide*, *The Pittsburgh Courier*, the *Baltimore Afro-American*, and the *Chicago Defender*. African Americans all over the country read these newspapers to learn about issues that could affect their lives. Rowan was shocked and angered to read about incidents of racial discrimination toward African American servicemen who were returning home from war.

Rowan's visit home was brief. His goal was to return to college and become a journalist. He earned a bachelor's degree at Oberlin College in Oberlin, Ohio. Then he attended journalism school at the University of Minnesota. While there, he worked as a freelance reporter covering the Minneapolis area for the *Afro-American*.

After graduating, Rowan was hired by the *Minneapolis Tribune*. He became one of the few African American reporters to work on a big-city newspaper. During this time, he suggested a daring story that would take him deep into the South.

In 1951, Rowan took a 6,000-mile journey through 13 Southern states. He sent back to the *Tribune* a series of articles entitled, "How Far from Slavery?" The articles described how he and other African Americans were treated. The series was inspired by a white Texan he had met in the Navy. The Texan had suggested that Rowan write about "all the little things it means being a Negro in the South, or anyplace where being a Negro makes a difference."

"How Far from Slavery?" described the segregation and poor conditions that African Americans in the South faced every day. It was an eye-opener for the readers of the *Minneapolis Tribune*. The series also brought Rowan wide recognition among important people in journalism, politics, and civil rights. "It set in motion a string of events that would change my life forever," he recalls.

Rowan's articles were praised in *Time* magazine, and won a Sidney Hillman Award for the best newspaper reporting in the nation that year. The award was given by a foundation set up by Hillman, a former textile union president, for the best articles about individual freedoms. It included a check for $500, six times Rowan's weekly paycheck. The articles also became the basis of his first book, *South of Freedom*. When Rowan returned to the South to write another series, titled "Jim Crow's Last Stand," he was honored with a Sigma Chi Award given by the Society of Professional Journalists.

A few years later, the U.S. State Department invited Rowan to travel to India and Southeast Asia to lecture on the importance of a free press. He reported on this issue for the *Tribune*, and won two more consecutive[2] Sigma Chi Awards.

---

2. **consecutive** (kuhn-SEHK-yuh-tihv) *adj.* following one after another

These were glamorous assignments. The most important stories of the time, however, were happening in the U.S. South. Rowan had reported on the beginnings of the Civil Rights Movement, including the Montgomery, Alabama, bus boycott and its leader, Dr. Martin Luther King, Jr. Rowan was often sought out for his insights[3] into the Civil Rights Movement.

Soon, Rowan's articles began to appear in newspapers and magazines around the country. In 1960, President John F. Kennedy made Rowan part of his administration. He sent him to negotiate[4] the top-secret agreements to free a U.S. pilot who had been shot down over the Soviet Union. In 1963, Kennedy chose Rowan to be U.S. Ambassador to Finland. He was the youngest ambassador, and only the fifth African American, to serve as an envoy.[5]

A few years later, President Lyndon Johnson appointed Rowan to be head of the United States Information Agency (USIA). This action made him the highest-ranking African American to serve in the federal government at the time.

In 1965, Rowan resigned from his USIA post to become a commentator[6] and syndicated[7] columnist. He reports on important events, such as the Civil Rights Movement. He is a familiar face to millions of Americans as a panelist on television news and political programs. Five days a week, he also broadcasts his radio program, "The Rowan Report." He and his wife, Vivien, live in Washington, D.C., and have three children. His columns appear regularly in major newspapers throughout the United States.

Rowan has written six books. His autobiography, *Breaking Barriers*, became a national best seller. In the book, he recalls

---

3. **insights** (ihn-SEYETZ) *n. pl.* clear understanding
4. **negotiate** (nih-GOH-shee-ayt) *v.* discuss or bargain to reach an agreement.
5. **envoy** (EHN-voy) *n.* a person sent by a government or ruler to transact diplomatic business
6. **commentator** (KAHM-uhn-tayt-uhr) *n.* a person who reports, analyzes, and evaluates news events or trends
7. **syndicated** (SIHN-duh-kayt-uhd) *adj.* appearing in several publications at the same time

Bessie Taylor Gwynn, the high school teacher who set him on the road to a life of journalism. Miss Bessie, as she was called, would tell her students, "If you don't read, you can't write, and if you can't write, you stop dreaming."

It is clear that Carl Rowan has never stopped dreaming—for a country that recognizes and values the contributions of its African American citizens.

> ***Did You Know?*** *During the 1880s, laws were created that made racial discrimination legal. They were called Jim Crow laws. The term comes from a song made popular by an African American dancer in the early 1800s. In the South, Jim Crow laws were used to deny African Americans the right to vote. Railroad cars, trolleys, and buses were segregated, as were water fountains and restaurants. African American children went to schools that were said to be "separate but equal." These schools were often in older buildings and had old textbooks that were passed down from students at white schools. During the Civil Rights Movement in the 1960s, the Jim Crow laws were repealed.*

AFTER YOU READ

EXPLORING YOUR RESPONSES

1. Rowan's experiences in the Navy forced him to "mature rapidly." What do you think maturity means?

2. Rowan was one of the first African American journalists to work for a big-city newspaper. How might you have felt if you had been in his place?

3. Rowan writes about issues that are important to him. If you were a journalist, what would you write about?

4. Rowan was influenced by articles he read in African American newspapers. How might a person be influenced by newspapers?

5. Rowan writes for newspapers, television, and radio. Which type of news media do you prefer? Why?

UNDERSTANDING WORDS IN CONTEXT

Read the following sentences from the biography. Think about what each underlined word means. In your notebook, write what the word means as it is used in the sentence.

1. Rowan was often sought out for his insights into the Civil Rights Movement.

2. [President Kennedy] sent him to negotiate the top-secret agreements to free a U.S. pilot who had been shot down over the Soviet Union.

3. In 1963, Kennedy chose Rowan to be U.S. Ambassador to Finland. He was the youngest ambassador . . . to serve as an envoy.

4. Rowan resigned from his USIA post to become a commentator. . . . He reports on important events, such as the Civil Rights Movement.

5. Rowan . . . [became] a <u>syndicated</u> columnist. . . . His columns appear regularly in major newspapers throughout the United States.

RECALLING DETAILS

1. How was Rowan's family affected by the Depression?

2. How did his commanding officer in the Navy expect white Southerners to react to Rowan?

3. Why was Rowan's acceptance into the Navy officer's training program notable?

4. What angered Rowan when he was discharged from the Navy?

5. What was the topic of Rowan's first series of articles for the *Minneapolis Tribune*?

UNDERSTANDING INFERENCES

In your notebook, write two or three sentences from the biography that support each of the following inferences.

1. Rowan's childhood experiences influenced his career.

2. As a young man, Rowan was determined to succeed.

3. "How Far from Slavery?" helped people see that African Americans and whites were not treated equally.

4. The main focus of Rowan's work is the status of African Americans in the United States.

5. Carl Rowan is not afraid to break down barriers.

INTERPRETING WHAT YOU HAVE READ

1. How do you think Rowan felt being the only African American in the Navy officer's training program?

2. How did Rowan help make changes in our society?

3. Why do you think President Kennedy made Rowan part of his administration?

4. Why do you think Rowan left his government post to continue his career in journalism?

5. Why do you think Carl Rowan named his autobiography *Breaking Barriers*?

ANALYZING QUOTATIONS

Read the following quotation from the biography and answer the questions below:

> *"When you are plucked out of a totally Jim Crow environment at age 17 and [are] thrown into a totally white environment where more is at stake than your personal life, you mature rapidly."*

1. What do you think it means to have "more at stake than your personal life"?

2. How might such an experience change a person?

3. How do you define maturity?

THINKING CRITICALLY

1. What experiences caused Rowan to be a journalist?

2. Why might people have consulted Rowan about the Civil Rights Movement?

3. What differences might you expect to find between newspapers written for different cultural groups?

4. How might being from a different cultural group change your life?

5. How does Rowan's life demonstrate the power of writing?

TONI MORRISON

Toni Morrison is shown with her novel *Beloved*, which won the Pulitzer Prize in 1988. Five years later, in 1993, Morrison became the first African American, and only the eighth woman, to win the Nobel Prize for literature.

When Toni Morrison was about 2 years old, her parents fell behind in the monthly $4 rent for their house in Lorain, Ohio. Angered, the landlord set fire to the house—while they were inside. Morrison describes the incident as "an out-of-the-ordinary, bizarre[1] form of evil. . . . For $4 a month, somebody would just burn you to a crisp."

It is a scene that could easily appear in one of Morrison's novels. Her novels are so powerful that Morrison achieved what is perhaps the greatest honor a novelist can earn. In 1993, Toni Morrison was the first African American, and only the eighth woman, to win the Nobel Prize for literature.

Morrison has known about creating dramatic stories since she was a small child. She was born Chloe Wofford in 1931, in Ohio, to a family that told stories as a daily part of life. She was the second of four children born to George and Ramah Wofford. The Woffords moved to Ohio from Alabama to escape racial violence. George Wofford was a shipyard welder who didn't graduate from high school. He had such pride in his work that when he welded a perfect seam, he welded his name onto the ship. Afraid that he might be out of work, he held three jobs at the same time for 17 years. Today, Morrison says her sense of pride and self-worth comes largely from her father.

When the Depression hit in the early 1930s, jobs became almost impossible to find. (See **Did You Know?** on page 29 for more information on the Depression.) Morrison began working part-time jobs to help out the family when she was 12. The family finally had to accept food from the government to survive. When Ramah Wofford found bugs in a sack of meal, she wrote a letter to President Franklin Roosevelt, asking for something better. Roosevelt's assistant ordered the local officials to give the

---

1. **bizarre** (bih-ZAHR) *adj.* extremely odd; unexpected

family better food. Her mother's letter taught Toni Morrison a lesson she now teaches others. Words can have enormous power.

Morrison took that lesson to heart. She was the only child in her first-grade class to start the year reading. As a child, she discovered a new world in books. This discovery led her to European novels by writers such as Jane Austen. What fascinated her was that although the writers described a world completely foreign to her, she was able to understand the characters. Today, people who read her novels say the same thing of her characters.

After high school, Morrison's family thought she would find work and get married. Instead, Morrison, who graduated with honors[2] from high school, decided to go to Howard University in Washington, D.C. There, she studied English literature and joined the college acting group. When she found that people had trouble pronouncing her name, she changed it to Toni.

After graduating from Howard, in 1953, Morrison went to Cornell University in Ithaca, New York. She earned her master's degree in English literature there in 1955. Morrison then took a job teaching at Texas Southern University in Houston. In 1957, she returned to Howard to teach. While there, she met and married Harold Morrison, a Jamaican architect.

In 1965, Morrison took a job in Syracuse, New York, as a textbook editor with Random House. In 1968, the company moved her to New York City, where she edited general interest books. She also worked for colleges and universities as a visiting professor. At night, she wrote. She wrote to battle loneliness. She also wrote because she felt no one was writing about the lives of African Americans. Nowhere in the literature she had read as a child, or was reading now, did she read about the lives of African Americans.

Morrison also began meeting with a group of other writers. She wrote a short story called "The Bluest Eye" for the group. It was about a young African American woman who longs for blue eyes. It was based on a conversation Morrison had when she was

---

2. **honors** (AH-nuhrz) *n. pl.* awards in recognition of academic achievement

a child. Like the subject of the story, the girl told Morrison that she no longer believed in God because she had prayed for blue eyes, and nothing had happened. The short story that Morrison wrote, about a young woman's longing for an acceptance she will never find, became a novel. It was published in 1970. The book was not a best seller, but it was praised for the beauty of its language. Reviewers also praised the novel's description of African American life.

Morrison continued writing, giving a voice to the experience of African Americans who continued to suffer racial prejudice.[3] *Sula*, published in 1973, focused on the long friendship of two African American women. The book was a Book-of-the-Month Club alternate selection.

In 1977, *Song of Solomon* brought Morrison literary fame. This book, about an African American man's journey to discover his past, captured readers' imaginations. Its lyrical[4] language and strong story won Morrison honors, such as the National Book Critics Circle Award. A year after its publication, 750,000 paperback copies of the book were in print.

Tar Baby was published in 1981, to more acclaim. Morrison became the first African American woman to appear on the cover of *Newsweek*. "Are you really going to put a middle-aged, colored lady on the cover of this magazine?" she joked.

In 1983, Morrison finally left her job at Random House to become a professor at the State University of New York at Albany. Four years later, she published the book that cemented her reputation, *Beloved*. It was based on a newspaper story about Margaret Garner, a woman who escaped from slavery in 1851. *Beloved* tells about a woman who killed one of her children and tried to kill two others. She calmly told police she would rather they die than live as slaves. In this novel, Morrison explores the way some African Americans reacted to slavery. Morrison

---

3. **prejudice** (PREH-juh-duhs) *n.* a negative opinion that has been formed without information
4. **lyrical** (LEER-uh-kuhl) *adj.* like a song

entices[5] readers into reading this shocking story with sentences as lovely as music. In 1988, *Beloved* won its author the Pulitzer Prize, one of the highest honors in American literature.

She followed this success with *Jazz*, a story about love and violence set in the 1920s in Harlem. In this work, Morrison makes clear the connection she feels between music—jazz in particular—and writing. In jazz, melodies travel unexpected paths. Odd notes creep in to surprise a listener. Morrison's writing is like that. It keeps the reader off-balance. Even though her novels are set in a specific world, it is a world that others can enter.

In May, 1993, Morrison was writing when a friend called her. "Did you hear?" the friend asked. Morrison was sure the news was bad. When she learned that she had won the Nobel Prize for literature, Morrison had a hard time believing it. Nobel Prizes are international awards given to people in many fields. Many consider them to be the most important awards in the world. When the Nobel committee called later that day, Morrison asked them to send her a fax. "Somehow, I felt that if I saw a fax, I'd know it wasn't a dream."

Morrison is at work on another novel. She has a home in Princeton, New Jersey, and has been a professor at the university there since 1989. She doesn't know when the novel will be finished. "There's something called novel time," she says. "It takes as long as it takes."

Morrison continues on the path she set for herself when she began writing. "Our silence has been long and deep," she says of African Americans. "We have always been spoken for. Or we have been spoken to." Today, she says, African Americans are telling their own story.

It is a story that contains anger and pain, but in Morrison's hands, the story of African Americans also involves hope. "At some point the world's beauty is enough," she writes in *Tar Baby*. "You don't need to photograph, paint, or even remember it. It is

---

5. **entices** (ihn-TEYES-uhs) *v.* attracts artfully

enough. No record of it needs to be kept and you don't need someone to share it with or tell it to. When that happens—that letting go—you let go because you can."

Morrison's writing contains scene after scene of the injustice that African Americans have always known. Those scenes give her work power. It is her nod to the world's beauty, and the possibility of love and freedom, that make certain that her work will live.

> **Did You Know?** While millions of Americans experienced financial disaster during the Great Depression of the 1930s, African Americans were hardest hit. Thousands of workers were laid off from their jobs by white employers who could no longer afford to pay someone to clean their homes. In clerical and semiskilled jobs, African Americans were dismissed three times more often than whites. Not until World War II, when the United States needed soldiers and workers to make products for the war, did African Americans begin to recover from the Depression.

AFTER YOU READ

EXPLORING YOUR RESPONSES

1. Morrison writes about the effects of racial prejudice. How has prejudice affected you or someone you know?

2. Morrison's father prided himself on a job that he did well, and showed this by welding his name onto a ship. Describe a time when you have been proud of a job you did well.

3. Morrison's interest in telling stories stemmed from childhood. Which of your interests can be traced to your childhood?

4. Morrison writes novels to tell about her experiences as an African American. In what other ways could people explain their experiences?

5. Toni Morrison was the first African American woman to win the Nobel Prize for literature. Discuss someone you admire who has also won fame for his or her work.

UNDERSTANDING WORDS IN CONTEXT

Read the following sentences from the biography. Think about what each underlined word means. In your notebook, write what the word means as it is used in the sentence.

1. Angered, the landlord set fire to the house—while they were inside. She describes the incident as "an out-of-the-ordinary, bizarre form of evil."

2. Instead, Morrison, who graduated with honors from high school, decided to go to Howard University in Washington, D.C.

3. She also kept writing, giving a voice to the experience of African Americans who continued to suffer racial prejudice.

4. Its lyrical language and strong story won Morrison honors, such as the National Book Critics Circle Award.

5. Morrison entices readers into reading this shocking story with sentences as lovely as music.

RECALLING DETAILS

1. How was Toni Morrison's family affected by the Depression?

2. Why did the Woffords move to Ohio?

3. How did Morrison learn about the power of words?

4. What examples did Morrison's father set that helped her later in life?

5. What steps did Morrison take to become a successful writer?

UNDERSTANDING INFERENCES

In your notebook, write two or three sentences from the biography that support each of the following inferences.

1. Morrison learned the power of words when she was a child.

2. The books Morrison read as a child influenced the books she later wrote.

3. Morrison did not fear hard work.

4. Morrison felt driven to write.

5. Morrison was deeply affected by racial prejudice.

INTERPRETING WHAT YOU HAVE READ

1. How might Morrison's father have helped her develop her sense of self-worth?

2. Why did Morrison's mother feel she deserved higher quality meal from the government, even though she didn't have to pay for it?

3. How might Toni Morrison's childhood have shaped her writing?

4. Why do you think many of Morrison's novels contain painful subjects?

5. Do you think Morrison's winning the Nobel Prize might cause people in her own country to look at her writing differently? Explain.

ANALYZING QUOTATIONS

Read the following quotation from the biography and answer the questions below.

> "Our silence has been long and deep," she says of African Americans. "We have always been spoken for. Or we have been spoken to."

1. What does it mean to be "spoken for . . . or spoken to"?

2. What do you think caused this silence? Explain your answer.

3. How might people learn to overcome such a silence?

THINKING CRITICALLY

1. What do you think Morrison learned from her parents?

2. In Morrison's first novel, *The Bluest Eye*, a young African American girl longs for blue eyes. How could this subject explore racial prejudice?

3. How could writing be like jazz?

4. Do you prefer reading about people who are like you, or different from you? Why?

5. How might words overcome prejudice?

CHARLES JOHNSON

Charles Johnson is pictured at the ceremony in which he won the National Book Award for his novel *Middle Passage*. Johnson was only the fourth African American writer to win the prize in its 40-year history.

"**I** have never been able to do things halfway, and I hungered—literally *hungered*—for life in all its shades and hues." These are the words of Rutherford Calhoun, the main character in Charles Johnson's novel, *Middle Passage*. They could also be the words of Johnson, a man whose thirst for new experiences has led him on some surprising journeys.

Charles Johnson was born in 1948, in Evanston, Illinois, a Chicago suburb, to Benjamin Lee Johnson and Ruby Elizabeth Johnson. Benjamin Johnson was a construction laborer and night watchman who sometimes worked weekends, as well as days and nights, to make ends meet. Johnson's mother had wanted to be a teacher. Instead, she worked as a maid at nearby Northwestern University, with her mother, who worked there as a cook. Ruby Johnson's poor health scuttled[1] her dreams of becoming a teacher. It also ended her chance to keep her job. Her asthma became so severe that she was forced to stay at home.

Instead of a classroom of students, Johnson's mother had one student, her son Charles. She packed the bookshelves of their home with hundreds of books. Then she taught her son to love reading them. When Johnson was 12 years old, his mother gave him his first diary. Johnson has kept a journal ever since.

When Ruby Johnson saw her son's talent for drawing, she arranged an introduction to Lawrence Lariar, an artist who also wrote mystery novels. Johnson, then 15, showed Lariar his work. Lariar convinced the boy that he had a future in cartooning. In 1965, two years after that meeting, Johnson sold his first illustrations to a magic company in Chicago. The company used the drawings to illustrate its catalog and paid him $12.

After he graduated from high school, Johnson majored in journalism at Southern Illinois University in Carbondale, Illinois.

---

1. **scuttled** (SKU-tuhld) *v.* destroyed; ruined

While there, he met the African American playwright and activist Amiri Baraka. Baraka's words about African American pride stirred something in Johnson. "Baraka said a black artist should bring his talent home to black people," Johnson says. "I cut classes for a week and just drew, all day, all night." As a result, Johnson drew hundreds of political cartoons that dealt with African American concerns. In the next five years, he sold nearly 1,000 cartoons to national and local publications. He also published two collections, *Black Humor*, in 1970, and *Half-Past Nation-Time*, in 1972.

Next, Johnson decided to be a philosopher.[2] In 1973, he earned a master's degree in philosophy at Southern Illinois University. At the same time, he worked as a photojournalist and wrote novels. He calls them "apprentice"[3] novels. "I wrote six novels in about two years because I didn't know any better," he says.

John Gardner, a professor at the university who was also a novelist, helped him focus his work. Gardner introduced Johnson to writers from times and places as different as ancient Greece and 14th century Europe. His reading took him in a direction opposite from Baraka's. In those early days of African American studies, Johnson says, there was a sense that "you didn't *need* to study European literature. . . . I just didn't feel comfortable with that." That narrow focus is "not something that a serious student of philosophy, or a serious artist, could really hold and create freely at the same time."

Johnson now wrote a seventh novel, *Faith and the Good Thing*. This one he sold to a publisher. In the novel, which was published in 1974, the main character, Faith Cross, goes in search of the "good thing"—truth. Faith's strange journey, in which she becomes different people while seeking truth, is "unlike anything else in a long time," one reviewer wrote.

---

2. **philosopher** (fuh-LAH-suh-fuhr) *n.* a person who tries to answer questions about the meaning of life
3. **apprentice** (uh-PREHN-tuhs) *adj.* one who is beginning to learn a trade or profession

Some reviewers noted that the novel was part philosophy, part fiction, and not really either. Johnson has heard that criticism from his philosopher friends, too. They tell him that "no novelist has ever done philosophy." His novelist friends, he says, tell him his "head gets in the way" when he tries to write a story. To Johnson, though, philosophy is at the heart of novels. Philosophy, he says, "is trying to conjure[4] sense out of the world, and if a story isn't doing that, then I don't know what it is doing."

In 1975, Johnson joined the faculty[5] at the University of Washington in Seattle. He also felt that it was time for another form of expression: screenwriting. He became interested in the story of Charlie Smith, who was then 135 years old. Smith was the oldest man in the United States. Johnson turned this story into the drama "Charlie Smith and the Fritter Tree." It appeared on the PBS series "Visions" in 1978.

Next on Johnson's growing list of achievements was the book *Oxherding Tale.* Despite having already published one book, Johnson had to send this novel to 20 publishers before Indiana University Press accepted it. "People had a hard time figuring it out," Johnson says. Readers told him, "It's funny, but it's about slavery, though it doesn't make *slavery* funny."

He published a book of short stories, *The Sorcerer's Apprentice,* in 1986. Again, readers told him that although the subject was African Americans, his attitude toward the subject was unusual. In one story, for example, an African American doctor meets a space alien and takes another look at his relationship with white America. Two years later, Johnson published *Being and Race: Black Writing Since 1970.* In this book, he argues that literature should not be judged on whether it has the attitudes toward race that are considered "correct" at the time.

In 1990, Johnson published the book that made his reputation. *Middle Passage,* like Johnson's other work, is surprising and complicated. It is about a freed slave named Rutherford

---

4. **conjure** (KAHN-juhr) *v.* to call up as if by magic; to create
5. **faculty** (FAK-uhl-tee) *n.* all of the teachers or professors at a school

Calhoun, who stows[6] away on a ship. He soon discovers that the ship is on its way to capture Africans, and send them to the United States and to slavery. Calhoun forms an uneasy relationship with the ship's mad, white captain. He finds, though, that he also feels uncomfortable with the Africans who are being taken to the United States, and to slavery. In the book, the Africans are portrayed as magical people who leave no fingerprints. Johnson worked on the book for six years. To research it, he says, "I went back and looked at every sea story"—everything from Sinbad to Homer to the accounts of enslaved people who talked about the journey from Africa. He studied dictionaries from the 19th century to understand the words people used then. He studied dictionaries of nautical[7] words.

The book was highly praised. "Charles Johnson manages to pack in more action and ideas than most novels three times its length," wrote *The Seattle Times*. "Long after we'd stopped believing in the great American novel, along comes a spell-binding adventure story that may be just that," wrote the *Chicago Tribune*.

Middle Passage won the National Book Award for 1990. That award is one of the most important awards for writing in the United States. It had been more than 40 years since the last African American man, Ralph Ellison, had been so honored. Suddenly, Johnson was being quoted as an expert on African Americans. He didn't like that one bit. "I find it very difficult to swallow the idea that one individual, black or white, can speak for the experience of 30 million people," he says. On the other hand, he did like the new readers he gained. "It's kind of overnight success after 20 years," he told an interviewer wryly.[8]

Johnson continues to teach at the University of Washington. He and his wife, the former Joan New, have been married since 1970. They have a son, Malik, and a daughter, Elizabeth. He also still writes.

---

6. **stows** (STOHZ) *v.* hides in a ship or airplane to gain free travel
7. **nautical** (NAWT-ih-kuhl) *adj.* having to do with the sea and ships
8. **wryly** (REYE-lee) *adv.* in a cleverly humorous way

Johnson believes that people need to explore as many parts of the world as they can. "Everyone ought to know as much as they can about as many cultures as they can," he says. "I personally think that everyone who knows about Lincoln ought to know about Frederick Douglass. . . . I don't believe in segregated education." (See **Did You Know?** below for more information about Frederick Douglass.)

Johnson has advice for schools. "I think that what schools need to do is teach the attitude of curiosity about the cultures of the world, so that you are a student for your whole life." Johnson is the right person to offer this suggestion. He has always followed his interests where they lead. They have led to writing that opens the world for his readers.

> **Did You Know?** *Like Charles Johnson's fictional character Rutherford Calhoun, Frederick Douglass was born a slave and eventually became a highly educated free man. Born in Tuckahoe, Maryland, in 1817, Douglass learned to read and write when he was 8 years old. In 1838, he escaped to New York. Douglass used his speaking and writing talents to publish newspapers and give lectures against slavery. Eventually, through public speaking, he raised enough money to buy his freedom. During the Civil War, he helped President Lincoln recruit African American soldiers.*

AFTER YOU READ

EXPLORING YOUR RESPONSES

1. Johnson has many interests. Do you think a person should concentrate on one career, or is it better to explore many different interests? Explain your answer.

2. Johnson believes everyone should be a student for life. How might someone benefit from being a student for life?

3. Johnson's mother was his teacher in his early years. Besides your teachers, who has helped you most with your education?

4. Johnson's book *Oxherding Tale* was rejected by several publishers. How can persistence be an advantage? How can it be a disadvantage?

5. Johnson enjoys studying a wide range of subjects. What subject would you like to learn about? Explain.

UNDERSTANDING WORDS IN CONTEXT

Read the following sentences from the biography. Think about what each underlined word means. In your notebook, write what the word means as it is used in the sentence.

1. Ruby Johnson's poor health scuttled her dreams of becoming a teacher.

2. He calls them "apprentice" novels. "I wrote six novels in about two years because I didn't know any better," he says.

3. Philosophy, he says, "is trying to conjure sense out of the world, and if a story isn't doing that, then I don't know what it is doing."

4. In 1975, Johnson joined the faculty at the University of Washington in Seattle.

5. It is about a freed slave named Rutherford Calhoun, who stows away on a ship.

RECALLING DETAILS

1. Name some of Johnson's interests.
2. What subjects did Johnson write about in his novels, and why?
3. How did Amiri Baraka's ideas influence Johnson?
4. Why did he change these ideas?
5. Describe *Middle Passage*.

UNDERSTANDING INFERENCES

In your notebook, write two or three sentences from the biography that support each of the following inferences.

1. Johnson is not afraid to take risks.
2. Johnson's mother had a great influence on his career.
3. Johnson and his character Faith Cross, in *Faith and the Good Thing*, share some ideas.
4. Johnson believes that all groups can learn from each other.
5. Being a "student for life" doesn't necessarily mean always learning in a classroom.

INTERPRETING WHAT YOU HAVE READ

1. What do you think Johnson learned from his father?
2. How could keeping a journal as a child have helped Johnson in his later life?
3. Why do you think Johnson pursued so many interests?
4. Why do you think Johnson became interested in Charlie Smith, the 135-year-old man?
5. Johnson believes that all creative work "tries to make sense out of the world." Explain how the artist who created one of your favorite movies, records, or pieces of art tried to make sense of the world.

ANALYZING QUOTATIONS

Read the following quotation from the biography and answer the questions below.

> *"Everyone ought to know as much as they can about as many cultures as they can," he says. "I personally think everyone who knows about Lincoln ought to know about Frederick Douglass. . . . I don't believe in segregated education."*

1. Why do you think that Johnson does not believe in segregated education?

2. How might learning about many cultures be helpful to a person?

3. Do you agree with Johnson? Explain.

THINKING CRITICALLY

1. In addition to writing, Johnson drew political cartoons. How do political cartoons convey serious messages? Use an example.

2. Why do you think it might be difficult to combine philosophy and novel writing?

3. Why do you think Johnson was so interested in the journey Africans took to become slaves in North America?

4. How might seeing the way Africans were being treated on the ship have affected Rutherford Calhoun?

5. How do you think Johnson would design a high school curriculum?

AUGUST WILSON

James Earl Jones and Mary Alice are shown in a scene from August Wilson's play *Fences*. Wilson received a Pulitzer Prize and a Tony award for the best play of the year for *Fences*. Wilson's aim in writing plays is to help people of all cultures see and understand African Americans.

High school was not easy for August Wilson. As the only African American student in a school in which, he says, "I didn't feel welcome, they wouldn't let me participate," he had frequent run-ins with other students. At another school, a ninth-grade teacher wrongly accused him of cheating on a term paper. The teacher demanded that Wilson prove he had actually written the 20-page research paper on Napoleon. Even though he pointed to his bibliography and footnotes, the teacher gave him a failing grade. Wilson was outraged. He walked out of the class and never returned. Decades later, he would become one of the most highly respected playwrights[1] in the United States.

August Wilson was born in Pittsburgh, Pennsylvania, in 1945, to Daisy and August Wilson. He lived with his mother, three sisters, and two brothers in a two-room cold-water apartment in one of the city's poorest neighborhoods. Daisy Wilson worked as a janitor. At times she was forced to accept welfare to support her family. Wilson's father, a white man who was a professional baker, did not live with the family.

Wilson learned to read at the age of 4. As he grew, he became a frequent visitor at Pittsburgh's excellent public libraries. When he was 12, he began to read the works of Richard Wright, Langston Hughes, Ralph Ellison, and other African American writers. He looked to these writers for inspiration.[2]

Always fascinated with words, Wilson wrote poetry and short stories. He listened to the way his neighbors spoke, and observed them in the street and in local businesses. "I think I got most of my information from these walking history books, the people themselves, who have gone through various experiences," he says.

1. **playwrights** (PLAY-reyets) *n. pl.* people who write dramas to be perfomed on stage
2. **inspiration** (ihn-spuh-RAY-shun) *n.* action or power that moves the intellect or emotions

When Wilson was 20, he worked as a cook and as a stock clerk. He used the money he earned to buy a typewriter, and used records of blues singers. (See **Did You Know?** on page 46 for more information on the role of the blues in U.S. music.)

Wilson was living in a run-down rooming house with an interesting assortment of people. His fascination with the blues enabled him to see how these people came to terms with the difficult lives they led. "I do think that the blues are the best literature we have as black Americans," he says.

Like many young African Americans, Wilson became politically active during the 1960s. He was involved in the Black Power Movement and considered himself to be a Black Nationalist. He became interested in playwriting because it enabled him to give life to the characters he created in his short stories. Wilson believed that "Black Americans have the most dramatic story of all mankind to tell." In addition, he established an activist theater company, Black Horizon, with a friend. The theater produced several of his early plays. Many of the plays that were written and produced at that time were powerful and angry.

In 1978, when Wilson was 33, he visited a friend who directed plays in the Minneapolis area. He liked that city so much that he left Pittsburgh and moved there. He also took a job writing scripts for exhibitions at the Science Museum of Minnesota.

Wilson devoted much of his time to writing plays, but he still enjoyed wandering around his new community, taking notes and observing the behavior of those around him. Now the location was Minneapolis, but his characters continued to use the expressions and patterns of speech that he had heard in his old Pittsburgh neighborhod.

Wilson admits that early in his playwriting career he had difficulty writing dialogue. "I couldn't write dialogue because I didn't value and respect the way in which black people spoke. I thought that in order to make art out of it, you had to change it. . . . I was forcing dialogue into the mouths of the characters instead of allowing them to say it themselves."

Wilson says that learning to write dialogue was a matter of writing down what he heard. "I don't think standing around those years in Pittsburgh hurt. . . . I began to hear the voices of those old men, just the way they thought and the way they spoke," Wilson recalls.

It was time to take his plays to a wider audience. Wilson submitted[3] several of his scripts to the Eugene O'Neill Theater Center, a national playwrights conference at Yale University in New Haven, Connecticut. Five were rejected, but he didn't give up.

Wilson found in his collection a recording made in the 1920s by blues singer Ma Rainey. This record inspired *Ma Rainey's Black Bottom*, the play that put Wilson's name in lights on Broadway. The title refers to a clog, or tap dance popular in the 1920s. The play focuses on a 1927 recording session with Ma Rainey, a woman considered to be the "mother of the blues."

Wilson's script for *Ma Rainey* was accepted and produced by the Yale Repertory Theatre. Several months later, in 1984, the play opened on Broadway. It garnered[4] praise from critics and theatergoers, and won the New York Drama Critics' Circle Award. *Ma Rainey* is the first in a series of Wilson's plays in which the characters deal with issues crucial[5] to African Americans. Each play is set in a different decade of the 20th century.

A few years later, *Fences*, Wilson's play about a Pittsburgh family, was seen by audiences in several regional[6] theater productions. The play was first produced at the Yale Repertory Theatre, then at theaters in Chicago, Seattle, and San Francisco. The production began with special readings at the O'Neill Theater Center. "We do four days of rehearsal and a very intensive workshop in which they hire actors and directors and a

3. **submitted** (suhb-MIHT-uhd) *v.* presented to others for consideration
4. **garnered** (GAHR-nuhrd) *v.* earned; collected
5. **crucial** (KROO-shul) *adj.* important; essential
6. **regional** (REE-juhn-uhl) *adj.* local; in one part of the country

[producer], and you sort of stand the play on its feet," says Wilson. This process helped Wilson sharpen the play's characters and themes.

Fences opened in 1987, and starred James Earl Jones. Jones played the role of Troy Maxson, an embittered[7] garbage collector and former Negro League baseball player, who tries to be a good family man. The play won several awards, including a Pulitzer Prize for the best play of the year. It also won a Tony award, the most important honor given a Broadway play.

Joe Turner's Come and Gone, The Piano Lesson, and *Two Trains Running,* all of which are set in Pittsburgh, have since had runs on Broadway. They have also been produced on stages around the country.

Wilson now makes his home in Seattle, with his wife, Judy. He has a daughter, Sakina Ansari, from an earlier marriage. He continues to write about the African American experience. "Suffering is only part of Black history. What I want to do is place the culture of Black America on stage . . . so that when you leave your parents' house, you are not in the world alone. . . . You have something that is yours, you have a ground to stand on, and you have a viewpoint."

Wilson believes that black and white people have similar experiences. "It's the same story," he says. "Although we do things differently, as blacks and whites, in America we all do the same things," he says. "We decorate our houses differently, we bury our dead differently. Almost everything—we do differently—but we also do [it] the same."

> **Did You Know?** *Blues music, or the blues, as it is called, originated in the late 1860s, after the Civil War. It began as "field hollers," which were solo calls and wails used among African Americans who worked on farms in the South. These field hollers were a form of communication among people who worked at great distances from one another. In the Mississippi Delta*

---

7. **embittered** (ihm-BIHT-uhrd) *adj.* made resentful or angry

region, the blues eventually became songs known as "country" or "down-home" blues. They were sung by male singers accompanied by a guitar. In the early 1900s, W.C. Handy, an African American band leader, composed blues songs known as "Memphis Blues" or "St. Louis Blues." By the 1920s, women singers, such as Ma Rainey, Bessie Smith, and Ethel Waters recorded the blues and brought them to a larger audience.

AFTER YOU READ

EXPLORING YOUR RESPONSES

1. About his experience at one high school, Wilson recalls, "I didn't feel welcome, they wouldn't let me participate." How could you help a student in that situation feel accepted?

2. When Wilson was 12, he began to read the works of African American writers. What could you do to learn more about your heritage?

3. The blues have greatly influenced Wilson's life. What is your favorite kind of music? How has it affected your life?

4. Words have always been important to Wilson. How can using words well help you reach your own goals?

5. Wilson's teacher gave him a failing grade on a paper on which he had worked hard. Who could you talk to if something like this happened to you? What would you say?

UNDERSTANDING WORDS IN CONTEXT

Read the following sentences from the biography. Think about what each underlined word means. In your notebook, write what the word means as it is used in the sentence.

1. Decades later, [Wilson] would become one of the most highly respected playwrights in the United States.

2. When he was 12, [Wilson] began to read the works of Richard Wright, Langston Hughes, Ralph Ellison, and other African American writers. He looked to these writers for inspiration.

3. It was time to take his plays to a wider audience. Wilson submitted several of his scripts to the Eugene O'Neill Theater Center, a national playwrights conference at Yale University in New Haven, Connecticut.

4. Several months later, in 1984, the play opened on Broadway. It <u>garnered</u> praise from critics and theatergoers, and won the New York Drama Critics' Circle Award.

5. *Ma Rainey* is the first in a series of Wilson's plays in which the characters deal with issues <u>crucial</u> to African Americans.

RECALLING DETAILS

1. Describe Wilson's high school years.

2. What role did books play in Wilson's life?

3. How does Wilson feel about the blues?

4. Why did Wilson become a playwright?

5. How did Wilson learn about writing dialogue?

UNDERSTANDING INFERENCES

In your notebook, write two or three sentences from the story that support each of the following inferences.

1. People in Wilson's high school treated him badly because he was African American.

2. Reading was important to Wilson from an early age.

3. Wilson learned to get what he wanted by working hard.

4. African American music has influenced Wilson's writing.

5. Wilson's plays help audiences understand African American life.

INTERPRETING WHAT YOU HAVE READ

1. Why do you think Wilson was attracted to the blues?

2. Why do you think Wilson described his neighbors in Pittsburgh as "walking history books"?

3. Wilson believes that "Black Americans have the most dramatic story of all mankind to tell." Why do you think he feels this way?

4. How did Wilson's love of words affect him as a young person, and as an adult?

5. Why do you think Wilson chose to have the characters in his plays deal with important African American issues?

ANALYZING QUOTATIONS

Read the following quotation from the biography and answer the questions below.

"I do think that the blues are the best literature we have as black Americans," [Wilson] *says.*

1. How are the blues and literature alike? How are they different?

2. Why do you think Wilson believes African American literature is important?

3. What story, movie, or song best tells a story that reflects your heritage?

THINKING CRITICALLY

1. Why do you think Wilson became a writer?

2. Before *Fences* opened, it was given special readings and workshops. How might that process help a writer revise a play?

3. Wilson said, "What I want to do is place the culture of Black America on stage . . . so that when you leave your parents' house, you are not in the world alone." What does this tell you about how he feels about his heritage?

4. How have reading and writing been important in Wilson's life?

5. How can reading and writing well help you in your own life?

CHARLAYNE HUNTER-GAULT

Charlayne Hunter-Gault is seated at her desk on the set of the PBS television show the "MacNeil/Lehrer NewsHour." Hunter-Gault has received many awards, including the George Foster Peabody Award for her work in television journalism.

Most newscasters simply report the news. Charlayne Hunter-Gault made it. A living, breathing history lesson, she can be seen weeknights on the Public Broadcasting System's (PBS) "MacNeil/Lehrer NewsHour." Not all her viewers realize that Hunter-Gault helped to change the course of history.

On January 9, 1961, Hunter-Gault walked onto the campus of the University of Georgia to register[1] for classes. Although she was only one student among thousands, it was as if she had climbed a tower and moved the school's clock forward two centuries. On this weekday morning, Hunter-Gault was joined by her mother and lawyer, and was surrounded by reporters and cameramen. Days before, on a Saturday morning, Hamilton Holmes had registered quietly. He and Hunter-Gault thus became the first African American students in the university's 175-year history.

It might have been only a fleeting moment, had Hunter-Gault been welcomed. Some whites were glad to see her, but they were afraid to say so. Instead, what Hunter-Gault remembers was a noisy and angry crowd of whites. Many yelled racial epithets.[2]

In the coming weeks, mobs set fires, burned crosses, and threw rocks. There was also a riot that state policemen refused to stop. Few people in that mob realized that Hunter-Gault was a lot like other young people. A long-time church member, she loved playing the piano and dancing. Like them, she had a loving family, too.

Her father had served in the Army as a chaplain[3] in World War II and the Korean War. Like many of the fathers and brothers of those in the crowd, Captain Hunter had risked his life for freedom. (See **Did You Know?** on page 56 for more information on African Americans in the armed forces.)

---

1. **register** (REH-juh-stuhr) *v.* officially enter a name onto a record or list
2. **epithets** (EH-puh-thehts) *n. pl.* insulting names
3. **chaplain** (CHA-plihn) *n.* a person who conducts religious services

Hunter-Gault remained composed on that day. She did not hide her face or show fear. She walked regally.[4] That's what the cameras captured: hatred and cruelty on the faces in the crowd, while center-stage a 19-year-old displayed a courage respected around the world.

Hunter-Gault credits her strength to the way she was raised. Though born in Due West, South Carolina, in 1942, she spent her early years in an African American neighborhood in Covington, Georgia. The area was called Rabbit Stew because early residents survived by catching rabbits for their food.

Although the African American citizens of Rabbit Stew were taxed like everyone else in Covington, there were no buses to take the children to schools, which were often miles away. The school buildings were broken down, classes were crowded, and there were few teachers. Most African Americans could not afford college. Textbooks were old and were usually discards[5] from the white schools. There were no cafeterias or science laboratories.

Still, adults in Rabbit Stew believed that the proper attitude, not material comforts, made the difference between success and failure. Contests were held to see which family could raise the most money for the school. The student of the winning family was crowned. The year that Hunter-Gault won, the "notion[6] that I was a queen took up residence in my head."

Even then, she says, "I wanted to be a journalist, a dream that would have been, if not unthinkable, at least undoable in the South of my early years. But no one ever told me not to dream, and when the time came to act on that dream, I would not let anything stand in the way of fulfilling it."

Her maternal grandmother, with whom Hunter-Gault's family shared a house for years, read three newspapers a day. Hunter-Gault especially enjoyed the *Brenda Starr* comic strip, which was about a female reporter. At night, she and her grandmother

---

4. **regally** (REE-guh-lee) *adv.* like a queen or king
5. **discards** (DIHS-kahrdz) *n. pl.* unwanted items
6. **notion** (NOH-shuhn) *n.* a theory or belief

listened to the news on the radio, and Hunter-Gault made up stories to tell her dolls and her two baby brothers.

Their father, who had graduated from a seminary,[7] was often away from home, serving as a chaplain on an Army base. After Hunter-Gault's tenth birthday, she and her mother and brothers moved to Atlanta, Georgia, a city in which many African Americans owned their own businesses. Two years later, the family joined Captain Hunter in Anchorage, Alaska.

Hunter-Gault hated leaving Atlanta, where she was known as having such a large vocabulary that she defended herself and her friends with words. In Alaska, she was the only African American student in her school, but this was not her only adjustment. Because of the inadequate education she had received in Georgia's segregated school system, she was academically behind her new classmates. Her father convinced her to stop worrying, saying that she had a superior mind. He was right. Eventually, Hunter-Gault excelled.

A year later, the family left Captain Hunter in Alaska and returned to Atlanta. Hunter-Gault edited the high school newspaper, and campaigned to be the 1959 homecoming queen. On the day of the election, she delivered school announcements over the public address system as usual. Then she added a campaign speech. Her ploy[8] worked. Once again, she was crowned queen.

Soon she would be a candidate for something far more important. In Topeka, Kansas, the family of an African American girl, Linda Brown, asked the U.S. Supreme Court to decide if it was constitutional to have separate schools for blacks and whites. In 1954, the court, ruling against Topeka's Board of Education, said that segregation in public schools was unconstitutional.

Hunter-Gault and Hamilton Holmes were encouraged by a group of African American leaders to test the court decision, in Georgia, by applying to the state university. It would take a

---

7. **seminary** (SEH-muh-ner-ee) *n.* an institution of higher education, often for studying to become a minister or priest
8. **ploy** (PLOI) *n.* a tactic used to frustrate an opponent

year-and-a-half for the legal team working for the National Association for the Advancement of Colored People (NAACP) to convince a Georgia judge to force the university to allow Hunter-Gault and Holmes to register. (See the biography of Ben Chavis on page 199 for more information on the NAACP.)

In the meantime, Hunter-Gault attended Wayne State University in Michigan. Early in 1961, she was admitted, by a judge's order, to the University of Georgia. When the student protests ended, Hunter-Gault settled down to a quiet existence. In 1963, she graduated with a degree in journalism. Hamilton Holmes graduated that same year, and eventually became an orthopedic surgeon.

Hunter-Gault would eventually work for the *New Yorker* magazine and *The New York Times*. In 1978, she joined the "MacNeil/Lehrer NewsHour" as its first woman anchor.[9] More recently, she has been a national correspondent for the show, reporting from locations as varied as South Africa and Bosnia. Sometimes she also interviews world leaders. Weekends, she anchors the network's weekly news show, "Rights and Wrongs."

Hunter-Gault has received numerous awards, including the George Foster Peabody Award, the highest honor in television journalism. She and her husband, Ronald Gault, have two children and live in New York.

Thirty years after her graduation, Hunter-Gault returned to the University of Georgia as another "first." This time she was the first African American in the school's history to deliver the graduation speech. During the speech, she read a letter from a white classmate who remembered seeing the mob advance toward the dorm. The student wrote, "For the first time I understood unreasonable cruelty. . . . I have tried since 1961 to treat all people with respect."

Hunter-Gault's attendance at the University of Georgia in 1961 changed not only the lives of African Americans. She also

---

9. **anchor** (ANG-kuhr) *n.* a person who introduces the stories of other television or radio journalists and remains in a fixed place, such as a studio

changed the lives of all Americans. Because of her courage, public universities around the United States began to open their doors to students of all cultural groups. Her success belongs to everyone.

Did You Know? *African Americans have distinguished themselves fighting in the Armed Forces to protect the ideals of the United States—even when freedom was not legally theirs. As long ago as the Revolutionary War, African Americans fought in major battles, including Valley Forge and Bunker Hill. In the Civil War, hundreds of thousands of runaway slaves joined the Union Army and helped to win the war against the South. In 1948, President Truman issued Executive Order 9981, which ended segregated units in the Armed Forces. African Americans have since risen to the highest ranks in the military.*

AFTER YOU READ

EXPLORING YOUR RESPONSES

1. When Hunter-Gault first arrived at the University of Georgia, she encountered racial epithets, mobs, cross burnings, and rock throwing. What might you have done in that situation?

2. Hunter-Gault moved several times when she was a child. How can a person adjust to a new home?

3. Hunter-Gault read newspapers and listened to news on the radio to prepare for her career in journalism. What might you do to prepare for a career?

4. Hunter-Gault used her large vocabulary to defend herself and her friends. How can words be used as defenses?

5. Hunter-Gault credits her strength to the fact that she was raised in a supportive family. How can a family help a person face difficult times?

UNDERSTANDING WORDS IN CONTEXT

Read the following sentences from the biography. Think about what each underlined word means. In your notebook, write what the word means as it is used in the sentence.

1. Instead, what Hunter-Gault remembers was a noisy and angry crowd of whites. Many yelled racial epithets.

2. She did not hide her face or show fear. She walked regally.

3. Textbooks were old and were usually discards from the white schools.

4. The year that Hunter-Gault won, the "notion that I was a queen took up residence in my head."

5. Then she added a campaign speech. Her ploy worked. Once again, she was crowned queen.

RECALLING DETAILS

1. Describe how Hunter-Gault was greeted by students at the University of Georgia.

2. What differences did Hunter-Gault find in her schools in Georgia and in Alaska?

3. Which Supreme Court ruling allowed Holmes and Hunter-Gault to register at the University of Georgia?

4. Describe Hunter-Gault's current job.

5. What did Hunter-Gault's white classmate learn during the unrest at the University of Georgia?

UNDERSTANDING INFERENCES

In your notebook, write two or three sentences from the biography that support each of the following inferences.

1. Hunter-Gault displayed courage in difficult situations.

2. Hunter-Gault's maternal grandmother had a strong influence on her desire to become a journalist.

3. The African American schools in Georgia were inferior to those in Alaska.

4. The residents of Rabbit Stew encouraged their children to succeed.

5. Hunter-Gault changed the lives of whites as well as blacks at the University of Georgia.

INTERPRETING WHAT YOU HAVE READ

1. Why did Hunter-Gault's advisors want her to register when the campus was full of students, and reporters had been notified?

2. How did Hunter-Gault prepare, even during her early years, to be a journalist?

3. How do you think life in Alaska was different from life in Atlanta for the Hunter family?

4. Hunter-Gault seized the opportunity and delivered a campaign speech over her high school intercom. What does this tell you about her?

5. What do you think Hunter-Gault's former classmate meant when he wrote, "For the first time I understood unreasonable cruelty"?

ANALYZING QUOTATIONS

Read the following quotation from the biography and answer the questions below.

> *"But no one ever told me not to dream, and when the time came to act on that dream, I would not let anything stand in the way of fulfilling it."*

1. What do you think Hunter-Gault meant when she said "no one ever told me not to dream"?

2. How did she fulfill her dream?

3. How can family or friends help a person "act on a dream"?

THINKING CRITICALLY

1. Why do you think Hunter-Gault wanted to be a journalist?

2. Why do you think some whites were afraid to tell Hunter-Gault that they were glad she'd enrolled at the University of Georgia?

3. What message do you think the state police gave when they ignored the riots on the university campus?

4. Why do you think African American leaders chose Hunter-Gault to test the new school integration law?

5. Why do you think the students at the University of Georgia ended their protest?

CULTURAL CONNECTIONS

Thinking About What People Do

1. Some experiences can change a person's career, way of thinking, or lifestyle. They are turning points in that person's life. Choose one writer from this unit and draw a time line of his or her life. Highlight one or two experiences that you consider to be turning points. Write a few sentences explaining how each turning point changed the person's life.

2. Imagine that you are one of the people in this unit. You have been invited to your school to speak about your experiences as an African American. Give a short speech about your successes and your frustrations.

3. Imagine that you are one of the writers in this unit, and write a "thank-you" note to someone who has influenced you. Mention several ways in which this person has helped you develop your career skills.

Thinking About Culture

1. Each of the writers in this unit feels strong ties to his or her heritage. Choose one writer and explain how that person's heritage has been important to him or her.

2. Most of the writers discussed in this unit had to endure many hardships. Choose two writers and explain how their hardships were similar and different. Use examples from the biographies.

3. What barriers or obstacles did these writers face because they are African American? Are some of these barriers common to other groups as well? Give reasons for your answers.

Building Research Skills

Work with a partner to complete the following activity.

Choose the person discussed in this unit whose work or life story interests you. Make a list of questions that were not answered in this biography. Your questions might include:

Hint: The Bibliography at the back of this book lists articles and books to help you begin your research.

☆ Who helped the writer develop his or her skills?

☆ How do the writer's personal experiences influence his or her work?

☆ How did the writer's family and friends support his or her career choice?

☆ How does the writer find ideas for his or her writing?

Hint: At the library, use the card catalog or computer data base to find books or articles by the writer and by other people who have written about that person's work.

☆ What style or styles does the writer use?

☆ What themes does the writer explore?

☆ What other writers have influenced his or her work?

☆ What can you learn about the African American experience from the writer's work?

Hint: As you read, jot down a few notes to help you remember details that interest you.

Next, go to the library to look for information that will answer your questions. Present your findings to the class in an oral report. You might include photographs of the writer or display his or her books.

Extending Your Studies

LANGUAGE ARTS **Your task:** *To write a play.* As you read in this unit, August Wilson is a playwright. What are the building blocks, or elements, of a play? Playwrights create *characters* who speak *dialogue.* They describe the *settings* where the action takes place, and write *stage directions* that tell the characters what to do and how to say their lines. The play's action is its *plot.*

Work with three or four classmates to write a play. When performed, your play should last five minutes or less, and should contain a part for each member of your group.

First, decide what you will write about. Brainstorm an idea, or try one of the following:

☆ Someone is trying to get a student in your school to use drugs. Write a play about how the student's friends step in to help. The play's dialogue may include arguments against using drugs.

☆ A new family has just moved into your neighborhood. The family's heritage is different from others in the neighborhood. Write a play about concerns the family might have, and how the neighbors might make the family feel welcome.

VISUAL ARTS **Your task:** *To create a chart that shows how a political cartoon comments on the news.* While studying journalism in college, writer Charles Johnson sold political cartoons to national and local publications.

Work with another student to choose a political cartoon and a news story that tells about the cartoon's topic. You may find a cartoon and matching article in a recent newspaper or on microfilm at the library.

Write a few paragraphs to tell other students about the political cartoon. Include answers to questions students may have, such as:

☆ In what part of the newspaper was the cartoon found?

☆ What do the pictures represent?

☆ How did the cartoonist use humor to get the point across?

Now draw your own political cartoon. Your cartoon's topic may come from world or national news, or from an event in your community or school. Work with your partner on the idea and caption for the cartoon.

To make the chart, assemble the newspaper cartoon and its matching news story along with your comments about the cartoon. Be sure to include the cartoon you created, too.

SOCIAL STUDIES **Your task:** *To conduct an interview.* Charlayne Hunter-Gault interviews world leaders, national political leaders, and other newsmakers.
Work with another student to interview someone who has affected your school or community in a positive, newsworthy way. Local newsmakers may include:

☆ a member of the community police, fire, or rescue squad

☆ a student at your school who is known for an achievement in sports, art, math, science, or writing

☆ a teacher who started a project that has helped students

Focus your questions on the person's achievement. Use the following questions as guidelines:

☆ Did your subject plan for the event, or was it a chance happening?

☆ Has the experience and/or publicity changed the subject's life?

☆ Would he or she do it again if the opportunity arose?

With your subject's permission, tape the interview with a cassette recorder or camcorder. (You may want to edit, or cut, parts of the interview before playing it for the class.) Then write a summary of what you have found. When you make your presentation to the class, use the summary as an introduction.

WRITING WORKSHOP

When a person writes about himself or herself, it is called an **autobiography**. In many ways, writing about yourself may not seem difficult. After all, who knows you better than you know yourself? Yet autobiographical writing can be challenging, too.

In this lesson, you will write an **autobiographical essay** about one event in your life that reveals something about your personality or attitude. In your essay, you will share your thoughts with your classmates. Another student will help you edit your work. Having someone else's point of view will help you ensure that your work makes sense and is enjoyable to read.

PREWRITING

Before you begin to write, think about your topic, organize your thoughts, and take notes. This first step in the writing process is called **prewriting**. You can use several different prewriting strategies to get started. Here are two suggestions:

Listing: On a blank sheet of paper, make three columns. Label the columns *People, Places,* and *Events.* Work quickly to fill in these columns, noting any memories that come to mind. For example, you might list a friend who has moved away, a cozy nook at your grandparents' home, or the time you got a kitten. List your ideas as they come to you, without worrying about order or spelling. When your page is filled, you will have many ideas for your essay.

Cluster Maps: Explore your topic further by creating a cluster map. To do this, choose one of the ideas or memories from your list and write it in the middle of a blank sheet of paper. Then think of as many images as you can that relate to that idea. Images should appeal to your sense of sight, smell, hearing, touch, or taste. As you create your cluster map, think about how these images reveal your point of view and thoughts.

Study the example below, in which the writer describes the first Kwanzaa she was old enough to remember. (Kwanzaa is a holiday that celebrates harvest time in Africa. It is honored by many African Americans.)

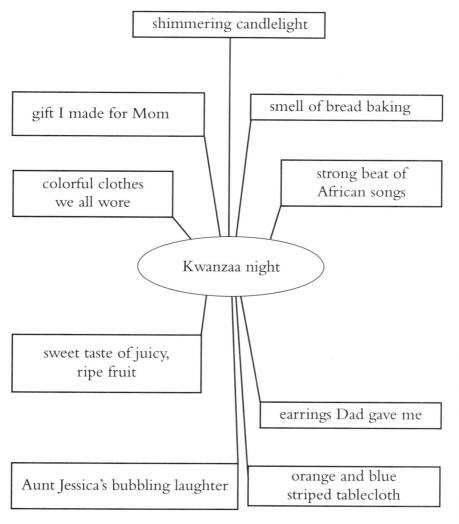

Look at your list and cluster one of your ideas. Jot down any additional details that will help your reader see you and your point of view.

Organize: Next, put your ideas in a clear and understandable order. You will probably write about your event chronologically, that is, in the sequence in which the events happened. Arrange your notes in the order in which you will use them.

DRAFTING

Now you can begin writing, or **drafting,** your autobiographical essay. You may want to keep the following strategies in mind as you write:

Use colorful language: Include vivid details that will appeal to your reader's senses of sight, hearing, smell, touch, and taste. Try to catch your reader by surprise at the beginning, and hold that interest. Be honest about yourself and the things you are writing about.

Use dialogue: Using the actual words of people adds life and variety to your writing. Choose words that help reveal your personality, and that of others, if you can.

Tell an exciting story: Do not worry about making your draft perfect. You will check for word usage and spelling errors later.

REVISING

Put your essay aside for a day or two. Then, with the help of another student who will act as your editor, evaluate and **revise** your work. See the directions for writers and student editors below.

Directions for Writers: Read your work aloud. Listen to how it flows. Ask yourself these questions:

☆ Is my writing clear?

☆ Are the ideas in order?

☆ Do the sentences make sense?

☆ Did I include interesting details?

☆ Have I drawn a picture of my event so my readers can see it in their minds?

☆ Have I shown my readers why this event was important to me?

Make notes for your next draft or revise your work before you give it to a student editor. Then ask the student editor to read your work. Listen carefully to his or her suggestions. If they seem helpful, use them to improve your writing when you revise your work.

Directions for Student Editors: Read the work carefully and respectfully, remembering that your purpose is to help the writer do his or her best work. Keep in mind that an editor should always make positive, helpful comments that point to specific parts of the essay. After you read the work, use the following questions to help you direct your comments:

☆ What did I like most about the essay?

☆ What would I like to know more about?

☆ Can I see the scene or event in my mind?

☆ Do I understand what the event means to the writer?

PROOFREADING

When you are satisfied that your work says what you want it to say, **proofread** it for errors in spelling, punctuation, capitalization, and grammar. Then make a neat, final copy of your autobiographical essay.

PUBLISHING

After you have revised your autobiographical essay, you are ready to **publish** it. Prepare a title page that includes your name as the author. Then add an illustration or graphic decoration to complete your "picture of yourself." Display your essay in a class Who's Who.

AFRICAN AMERICANS IN THE FINE AND PERFORMING ARTS

In this unit, you will read about some African Americans who made a difference in the fine and performing arts. As you read the unit, think about what makes each of these people unique. Think, too, about some of the qualities that helped them become successful. In what ways did hard work and determination help them succeed in their fields?

Actor **Denzel Washington**, who played Malcolm X in the movie of that name, says that hard work is necessary to achieve a goal. "Learn your history," he advises. "Take the time and effort to find out who you are."

For dancer **Judith Jamison**, the key to success is positive thinking. "So many people dwell on negativity and I've survived by ignoring it. It dims your light and it's harder each time to turn the power up again."

Jacob Lawrence's paintings often explore the many difficulties African Americans have endured. "There was conflict and struggle," he says. "But out of the struggle came a kind of power and even beauty."

Photographer **Lorna Simpson** also reflects on the experience of being African American. Her work, she says, often comments on slavery and "my contemporary connection to it."

Jazz musicians **Branford** and **Wynton Marsalis** have won their fame through hard work. As Wynton says, "Kids always ask, 'How were you discovered?' and I say, 'Man, when *I* discovered the practice room.' You won't get anywhere without sweat."

As you read these biographies, think about the drive that each person displayed in pursuing his or her art, despite discouragement and hardships.

DENZEL WASHINGTON

Denzel Washington holds the Oscar he won for Best Supporting Actor in the 1990 movie *Glory*. Washington feels that there has been too much stereotyping in movies and television, so he only accepts roles that show African Americans in a positive light.

Actor Denzel Washington had six weeks to prepare for the role of Stephen Biko. Biko was a young South African activist who had been murdered for his stand against that country's apartheid[1] system. First, Washington read about Biko in books, newspapers, and magazines. He watched videotapes of Biko. He spoke with people who actually knew the man. Then Washington began to change his appearance so that he looked like Biko. He gained 30 pounds. He removed the dental caps from his teeth. He grew a mustache and a goatee. Finally, he developed a South African accent. His intention[2] was to make audiences believe that he *was* Stephen Biko in the film *Cry Freedom*.

Washington often changes the way he looks, speaks, or moves to create a character for a movie or a play. During the filming of *Cry Freedom*, Washington, acting as Biko, delivered a speech before a large crowd of African people who had been hired as extras.[3] When he finished, the crowd burst into long applause. "That's when I felt closest to [achieving] what I was after," Washington says. For this role, he received an Academy Award nomination for best supporting actor.

Denzel Washington was born in 1954, the second of three children. His mother, Lennis, was a former gospel singer who owned several beauty parlors. His father, Denzel, Sr., was a Pentecostal[4] minister. He was raised in Mount Vernon, New York, a multiracial suburb of New York City. "My friends were West Indians, blacks, Irish, Italians, so I learned about a lot of different cultures," he recalls. Washington would later put to use

---

1. **apartheid** (uh-PAHR-teyet) *n.* the former South African policy of strict racial segregation and discrimination against non–whites
2. **intention** (ihn-TEHN-shuhn) *n.* determination to act in a certain way
3. **extras** (EHK-struhs) *n. pl.* people hired to act in a group scene in a motion picture
4. **Pentecostal** (pehnt-ih-KAWS-tuhl) *n.* form of Christian faith that emphasizes revivalist worship

his friends' gestures and ways of speaking to help him create stage and film characters.

He describes his father as a man who taught his children about integrity,[5] hard work, and responsibility. Denzel Washington, Sr., rarely allowed his children to go to the movies unless they were going to see Biblical or Walt Disney films. His parents divorced when he was 14. Washington credits his mother, who raised him, for keeping him out of trouble and off the streets. "My mom's love for me, and her desire for me to do well, kept me out of trouble," he says.

When Washington went through a rebellious period, Lennis Washington enrolled her son in a boy's prep school in upstate New York. He was a star athlete there. He played on the school's football and baseball teams, and also ran track.

Almost by accident, Washington discovered that he had a talent for acting, too. While working as a summer camp counselor, he took part in the staff talent show. He enjoyed that experience so much that he signed up for a theater workshop during his junior year at Fordham University in the Bronx, New York. Soon he was acting in student productions of Shakespeare's *Othello* and Eugene O'Neill's *Emperor Jones*.

Also while he was in college, Washington landed a part in *Wilma*, the made-for-television movie about Olympic track star Wilma Rudolph. After graduation, he spent a year at the American Conservatory Theatre in San Francisco.

Washington is one of the most sought-after actors today because of the respect he has for the characters he portrays. He has always turned down roles that show African Americans in a negative light. This was true even when he first started acting. "There is so much negativity and greed, doing things for the dollar, exploitation[6] for ratings," he says. As a young actor he needed money, but he was not willing to accept roles that he found offensive.[7] Instead, he signed up to work as a recreational

---

5. **integrity** (ihn–TEHG–ruht–ee) *n.* a code of high moral or artistic values
6. **exploitation** (ehks–ploi–TAY–shuhn) *n.* to make immoral use of something for profit
7. **offensive** (uh–FEHN–sihv) *adj.* giving painful or unpleasant sensations

counselor. Fortunately, he was hired for an important off-Broadway play two weeks later.

An actor can spend months, even years, waiting to be chosen for a role in a play or movie. African American actors often have a particularly difficult time because there are fewer roles for them in major film or theater productions. (See **Did You Know?** on page 74 for more information about the 19th-century African American actor, Ira Aldridge.) To avoid being unemployed, many have had to take parts that are negative and stereotypical,[8] such as drug dealers and criminals.

The characters that Washington portrays tend to be men of good conscience[9]—those who want to do the right thing. They are often people most of us would like to have as next-door neighbors. In 1982, Washington became a familiar face to millions of viewers as Dr. Phillip Chandler in the TV series "St. Elsewhere." The show ran for six years, giving people on both sides of the camera a chance to appreciate Washington's talent.

In 1984, Washington was offered the role of an outspoken young Army private in the movie *A Soldier's Story*. The film is about racial tensions on a U.S. Army base during World War II. Washington had already played the role in a stage production several years before.

Other roles followed: the principal of a drug-infested inner-city high school in *The George McKenna Story*; a jazz musician in *Mo' Better Blues*; a police chief on a Caribbean island in *The Mighty Quinn*; a runaway slave in the 1989 Civil War film *Glory*, for which he won an Academy Award; and a lawyer who defends the rights of another lawyer with AIDS in *Philadelphia*.

Washington has asked filmmakers to offer him roles that might have gone to white actors. He can do this because he has strong box office appeal for both white and black audiences. His roles in the movies *The Pelican Brief*, in which he plays a reporter, and *Much Ado About Nothing*, in which he plays a wealthy landowner, are examples.

---

8. **stereotypical** (stehr-ee-uh-TIHP-ihk-uhl) *adj.* not original or individual
9. **conscience** (KAHN-shuhns) *n.* a knowledge or sense of right and wrong

Yet it is Washington's powerful portrayal of Malcolm X, in the film of the same name, for which he will be remembered for many years. The film was produced and directed by African American filmmaker Spike Lee. "I'm not Malcolm X," Washington says. "But the same God that moved Malcolm X can move me. This is a story about the evolution of a man. . . . My prayer is to illustrate that and have that be some kind of healing for people."

Although Washington has become one of Hollywood's most successful leading men, he insists, "I am not a movie star!" Off the screen, he is able to walk the streets without being recognized.

He lives quietly in Los Angeles with his wife, Pauletta Pearson, who is an actress and a professional musician. The couple has four children. When he is not making a movie on location, Washington spends his time with his family, attending church, and coaching his children's Little League teams.

He is also involved with the Negro Ensemble Company (NEC), a theater group in New York City, where he trained early in his career. Washington believes, "It's our responsibility as African Americans, and as entertainers who have had some success and have come through NEC, to lend a hand to help . . . [the company that] made us what we are."

Denzel Washington is aware of the impression that he can make on the minds of young people. "I love feeding them with positive energy," he says. Quoting Malcolm X, Washington believes that many youngsters have been taught that African Americans have never done anything and can never do anything. But he advises them to "Learn your history. Take the time and effort to find out who you are."

> **Did You Know?** In 1821, African Americans in New York City established their own theater, the African Grove. An actor who may have appeared on the stage of that theater was Ira Aldridge. The son of a New York minister, Aldridge learned to act at the city's African Free School. He left the United States because racial prejudice

limited roles for African American actors. He moved to Europe in 1925, where he became the first African American actor to gain fame in the Western world. Aldridge received medals from the kings of Prussia and Austria for portraying Shakespeare's Othello. *When Aldridge was hired to act in a play in Baltimore, Maryland, some people were upset that he would appear on the same stage as white actors. As a result, he never appeared in a major role in the United States.*

AFTER YOU READ

EXPLORING YOUR RESPONSES

1. Washington's acting style was influenced by his childhood friends. In what ways are people influenced by their childhoods?

2. Washington refused to take acting roles that show African Americans in a negative light. If you were an actor, what roles would you accept? Why?

3. Washington discovered his talent for acting almost by accident. How did you discover a talent you have?

4. Washington credits his mother for keeping him out of trouble. How can family members help one another?

5. Washington prepared extensively for his roles as Stephen Biko and Malcolm X. How do you prepare for something important that you have to do?

UNDERSTANDING WORDS IN CONTEXT

Read the following sentences from the biography. Think about what each underlined word means. In your notebook, write what the word means as it is used in the sentence.

1. His intention was to make audiences believe that he *was* Stephen Biko in the film *Cry Freedom*.

2. He describes his father as a man who taught his children about integrity, hard work, and responsibility.

3. "There is so much negativity and greed, doing things for the dollar, exploitation for ratings."

4. To avoid being unemployed, many [actors] have had to take parts that are negative and stereotypical, such as drug dealers and criminals.

5. The characters that Washington portrays tend to be men of good <u>conscience</u>—those who want to do the right thing.

RECALLING DETAILS

1. How did Washington prepare to play Stephen Biko?
2. How did Washington discover that he had a talent for acting?
3. Why do African American actors have difficulty finding roles?
4. What types of acting roles does Washington choose? Why?
5. How does Washington think learning history can help African Americans?

UNDERSTANDING INFERENCES

In your notebook, write two or three sentences from the story that support each of the following inferences.

1. Washington believes that a key to good acting is understanding the character you are playing.
2. Washington's life and career reflect his parents' ideals.
3. Filmmakers now accept Washington on his own terms.
4. Washington takes on a wide range of parts.
5. Washington has not forgotten the people who helped him get where he is.

INTERPRETING WHAT YOU HAVE READ

1. Why did Washington enjoy the role of Stephen Biko?
2. How do you think Washington's choice of characters was influenced by his upbringing?
3. Why did Washington turn down roles that portray African Americans as drug dealers or criminals?
4. How has Washington's respect for the characters he portrays helped his career?

5. Why do you think Washington continues to be involved with the Negro Ensemble Company?

ANALYZING QUOTATIONS

Read the following quotation from the biography and answer the questions below.

"There is so much negativity and greed, doing things for the dollar, exploitation for ratings."

1. What does it mean to "do things for the dollar"?

2. Do you agree with Washington's judgment? Explain.

3. How would you respond if you were forced to choose between an opportunity to make money, and standing up for what you believe in?

THINKING CRITICALLY

1. Choose one of the characters Washington has played. Why might he have chosen that role?

2. Do you agree or disagree with Washington's decision not to take on roles that portray African Americans in a negative light? Explain.

3. Why do you think Washington's movies are popular?

4. What does it mean to be a person of good conscience?

5. Do you think it is good for an actor's career to take only certain types of roles? Explain.

JUDITH JAMISON

Judith Jamison (center) rehearses for a benefit performance at City Center in New York City for the Alvin Ailey American Dance Theater. With her are Lazaro Carreno (left) and Maria Llorente (right), prize-winning dancers from the National Cuban Ballet. Jamison now teaches students her award-winning style.

After 16 minutes of dancing that stretched her body, her mind, and her heart, Judith Jamison collapsed on the stage. The audience exploded in cheers and screams. Everyone expected memorable dancing from Jamison, but when she first danced *Cry*, people were stunned. Jamison had taken the theme of the dance—the historical journey of African American women—and made it a cry of love, strength, and courage. "Judith Jamison is no ordinary dancer," wrote Clive Barnes for *The New York Times*. "Now Alvin Ailey has given his African queen a solo that wonderfully demonstrates what she is and where she is."

It was another triumph for the dancer who was once considered too tall and "too African American" to be a ballet star. But Judith Jamison turned those perceptions[1] into strengths. She used her long legs to make spectacular leaps. She pulled herself up to her full 5'10" height and moved across the stage in strides. She was show-stopping.

Jamison credits her upbringing for a self-confidence that helped her believe in herself when others did not. She was born in 1943, in Philadelphia. Her parents had moved there from the South as part of the migration of African Americans that began in the 1940s. (See **Did You Know?** on page 84 for more information about the migration north of African Americans at this time.)

Jamison's father, John Henry Jamison, worked as a sheet metal engineer. Her mother, Tessie Belle Jamison, cared for Judith and her brother Johnny, who was three years older than Judith. The children grew up with rules. "We weren't loud," Jamison says. "We only spoke when we were spoken to by an elder." Jamison's mother cooked every meal. Her father made most of their furniture by hand. The family was active in church.

---

1. **perceptions** (puhr-SEHP-shuhnz) *n. pl.* beliefs; mental images

The arts were an important part of Jamison's childhood. There was always music in the house. Her father sang to her in his deep baritone and taught her to play classical piano. The sounds of opera on the radio filled Saturday afternoons. "Philadelphia was full of wonderment for me as a child, full of people interested in artistic expression," Jamison says.

As a child, Jamison remembers standing out. "When I was 6 years old I was tall, lean, and long-legged. At 10 I could walk down the street and see everybody's head," she says. "It's not that I felt especially tall. I was wondering when everybody else was going to catch up." Also when she was 6, Jamison began dance lessons. Her teacher, Marion Cuyjet, remembers being astonished at this tall girl's grace and ability. "I was so excited by her that all my husband and I talked about on Saturday nights, the only night I had dinner home, was Judi," she says.

Jamison also excelled at physical activity at school. She still remembers the sting of being placed in the back row in a gymnastics performance. "I felt that I was being put in the back row because I was Black," she writes. "I knew I was good. There was no one on that stage doing this work better than I. I was angry, but I knew even then how to direct my anger." Jamison performed her heart out.

After graduating from high school, Jamison was unsure of what do to. Finally, Marion Cuyjet convinced her to go to Fisk University in Nashville, Tennessee, a historically black college. After three semesters at Fisk, Jamison transferred to the Philadelphia Dance Academy. While she was there, in 1965, the legendary[2] dancer Agnes de Mille saw Jamison dance. "There were just the ordinary students, some good, some bad, with this one astonishing girl," de Mille said. She asked Jamison to go to New York to be in a new production for the American Ballet Theatre. Jamison was thrilled. "I had pictures of the dancers all over my bedroom wall," she says.

Jamison went to New York and danced in *The Four Marys*.

---

2. **legendary** (LEHJ-uhn-dehr-ee) *adj.* relating to a legend; famous

Critics praised her performance, and she decided to stay in New York. Dancing work was scarce, though, and Jamison began to work as a clerk to support herself. This big, rangy[3] dancer was not the ballerina many dance companies were looking for. She was not small and white. None of that fazed[4] Jamison. "So many people dwell on negativity and I've survived by ignoring it," she has written. "It dims your light and it's harder each time to turn the power up again."

When she found out about a dance audition for a TV show, Jamison went. She wore pink ballet shoes and a leotard. The others were wearing more sophisticated[5] clothes. Jamison failed miserably. With little time to practice, her skills had become rusty. She was asked to leave. She left the audition in tears.

Three days later, a man who had seen that audition called her. He liked what he had seen, despite Jamison's problems. The man was Alvin Ailey. He asked Jamison to join his dance group. Without hesitation, she said yes. It was to become a remarkable association that lasted until Ailey's death. Ailey choreographed.[6] Jamison added a dancing spirit that stirred audiences.

Ailey's group, the Alvin Ailey American Dance Theater, became better known abroad than in the United States. Jamison tells about their trips to such places as Egypt, Austria, and Germany. They ran out of money in Barcelona, Spain. They ran out of food in Russia. They found themselves in the middle of a war in the Congo, in Africa. They danced on wet floors, during lightning storms, and on a stage that hadn't been opened in 40 years. "We had faith in Alvin," Jamison says. "He believed his dancers had to keep going, no matter what."

In 1971, Ailey choreographed *Cry* for Jamison. It became her signature[7] piece. Jamison's grandmother saw her perform the

3. **rangy** (RAYN-jee) *adj.* slender and long-limbed
4. **fazed** (FAYZD) *v.* disturbed; stopped
5. **sophisticated** (suh-FIHS-tuh-kayt-uhd) *adj.* worldly-wise
6. **choreographed** (KOHR-ee-uh-graft) *v.* arranged or directed a dancer's moves
7. **signature** (SIHG-nuh-chŏŏr) *adj.* identified with a person

dance in Philadelphia. "She hadn't seen me dance since I was 8 years old, and I wanted to give the performance of my life. I remember feeling and thinking that the dance was like a transfer of spirit from my grandmother to my mother to me."

The next year, Jamison was presented with the *Dance Magazine* award. "I'd like to say something about Judith, who is an extraordinary person in American dance, in the history of dance," said Alvin Ailey at the ceremony. "Judith is a lady who came in 1965 to my company, a tall, gangly[8] girl with no hair. I always thought she was beautiful. Judith has developed, she has grown; she's a beautiful, extraordinary person."

Jamison was moving toward the pinnacle[9] of her career as a dancer. She posed for fashion magazines. She performed with Mikhail Baryshnikov, one of the best-known male ballet dancers in the world. She danced in 70 different ballets for Alvin Ailey. In 1984, Jamison was offered a role in the Broadway musical *Sophisticated Ladies.* "I wanted to try something else," Jamison explains. "I gave up safety and jumped into Broadway."

Although Ailey was hurt, he accepted Jamison's departure. He also encouraged her to start choreographing. She enjoyed it. "It's a blessing to be able to transfer your inner thoughts and your emotions to other people, who then relay your message to an audience."

In 1988, Jamison began the Jamison Project. "I wanted to explore the opportunities of getting a group of dancers together," she says. She loved the energy, and the chance to put her own ideas on the stage. At the same time, she was helping Ailey, who was sick. Jamison was a guest artistic associate for Ailey's company in 1988-89, and helped to produce a PBS special featuring the company. Soon after, Jamison began work on her own TV special, "The Dancemaker: Judith Jamison."

Seven months before he died, in December of 1989, Ailey asked Jamison to take over the company. "The Jamison Project

8. **gangly** (GAN-glee) *adj.* loosely and awkwardly built
9. **pinnacle** (PIH-nih-kuhl) *n.* the highest point

was an extraordinary group of people who worked well together," she says. "But there was no way I could have refused Alvin." For six months after his death, she ran both the Jamison Project and the Alvin Ailey American Dance Theater. Then she closed the Jamison Project.

Jamison idolized[10] Ailey. "I don't feel as though I'm standing in anyone's shoes," she has said. "I'm standing on Alvin's shoulders." Jamison brought new energy to Alvin Ailey's company. In 1993, the company performed at President Clinton's inauguration.

Jamison continues to choreograph. She also shares the knowledge she has gained from dancing for so long. "Feel free to make mistakes in class and stumble in class, but learn your craft," she tells new dancers. "Learn the craft of knowing how to open your heart and how to turn on your creativity. There's a light inside of you." The light shines from Judith Jamison as well, shining from a woman who believes in herself enough to let her spirit dance.

> ***Did You Know?*** *During the 1940s, 1950s, and 1960s, more than four million African Americans moved from the South to the North. They moved because farm jobs disappeared as new machinery replaced people. Until that time, farm work had been the main source of jobs in the South. In the North, African Americans found work in factories in big cities. In 1940, less than half of African Americans lived in cities. By 1987, 86 percent of African Americans lived in or near cities.*

---

10. **idolized** (EYED-uhl-eyezd) *v.* worshipped

AFTER YOU READ

EXPLORING YOUR RESPONSES

1. Jamison's parents were fans of opera and classical music. What type of music do you enjoy? Explain.

2. Although she failed in her audition, Jamison did not give up. Do you think it is always good to keep trying, even when you do not succeed at first? Why?

3. Alvin Ailey gave Jamison a start as a professional dancer. What career are you considering?

4. Jamison's group performed at President Clinton's inauguration in 1993. What kinds of performances do you think a president should host? Why?

5. Jamison gave up her own company because Alvin Ailey asked her to run his. Do you think there is a limit to how much friends should help each other? Explain.

UNDERSTANDING WORDS IN CONTEXT

Read the following sentences from the biography. Think about what each underlined word means. In your notebook, write what the word means as it is used in the sentence.

1. It was another triumph for the dancer who was once considered too tall and "too African American" to be a ballet star. But Judith Jamison turned those perceptions into strengths.

2. This big, rangy dancer was not the ballerina many dance companies were looking for. She was not small and white. None of that fazed Jamison.

3. She wore pink ballet shoes and a leotard. The others were wearing more sophisticated clothes.

4. In 1971, Ailey choreographed *Cry* for Jamison. It became her signature piece.

5. Jamison was moving toward the pinnacle of her career as a dancer. She posed for fashion magazines. She performed with Mikhail Baryshnikov, one of the best-known male ballet dancers in the world.

RECALLING DETAILS

1. Describe Jamison's childhood.

2. Why was Jamison rejected at her audition?

3. How did Alvin Ailey and Jamison meet?

4. What did Jamison do when she left Ailey's troupe?

5. Why did Jamison close her dance company?

UNDERSTANDING INFERENCES

In your notebook, write two or three sentences from the biography that support each of the following inferences.

1. Jamison's parents' interests probably influenced her choice of career.

2. Jamison is not easily discouraged.

3. Ailey and his dancers were committed to the company.

4. Jamison spent her years away from the Ailey troupe trying new ventures.

5. Jamison believes that students should test their abilities.

INTERPRETING WHAT YOU HAVE READ

1. How do you think Jamison's career was affected by the fact that she did not look like other ballerinas?

2. What do you think Ailey liked about Jamison's dancing at her audition?

3. How did Jamison's heritage influence her dancing?

4. Why do you think Ailey asked Jamison to return to run his company when he was sick?

5. Why might Jamison want dancers to make mistakes in class?

ANALYZING QUOTATIONS

Read the following quotation from the biography and answer the questions below.

> [Jamison's grandmother] "hadn't seen me dance since I was 8 years old, and I wanted to give the performance of my life. I remember feeling and thinking that the dance was like a transfer of spirit from my grandmother to my mother to me."

1. What do you think Jamison meant when she said the dance "was like a transfer of spirit"?

2. What does this quotation tell you about Jamison's relationship with her grandmother?

3. What are the most important things that one generation can pass on to the next?

THINKING CRITICALLY

1. *The New York Times* said that *Cry* demonstrated "what [Jamison] is and where she is." What does this mean?

2. How can dancing show strength and courage?

3. Jamison's parents supported her goal in many ways. How can the support of others help a person?

4. Why was Jamison's self-confidence as important as her talent?

5. Why do you think Alvin Ailey's American Dance Theater was better known in other countries than in the United States?

JACOB LAWRENCE

Jacob Lawrence's paintings, like the one above, titled *Dreams Number 2*, explore his pride in his heritage. Lawrence celebrates the conflict and struggle, but also the power and beauty of the African American experience in his work. He is one of the best-known painters in the United States today.

The invited guests gathered in groups in front of the paintings. Many were visibly moved by what they saw. Some even wiped away tears.

In one painting, titled *And they were very poor*, a sharecropper[1] and his wife sit at a table staring at empty bowls. An especially chilling painting was titled *Another cause was lynching. It was found that where there had been a lynching, the people who were reluctant to leave at first left immediately after this.* This painting depicted a lynching by showing an empty hangman's noose above bare earth, and the figure of a woman bent over in grief. Another painting, titled *And the migration spread*, showed African Americans cramming themselves onto an overcrowded railroad car, desperate to escape from poverty and persecution.

On that cool, fall evening in 1993, several hundred guests who were invited to the elegant 19th-century mansion also pressed around a quiet, dignified man in his 70s. They were eager to meet the guest of honor, Jacob Lawrence, an African American who is one of America's greatest living painters.

On exhibit that evening at the Phillips Collection in Washington, D.C., was a series of 60 paintings by Lawrence titled, *The Migration of the Negro*. This series portrays the great migration of African Americans that occurred in the early part of this century.

Lawrence was not involved in this migration, but his parents had moved north from South Carolina to find what they hoped would be a better life. Rose Lee and Jacob Lawrence, Sr., who was a railroad cook, settled in Atlantic City, New Jersey. Lawrence was born there in 1917.

When Lawrence's father deserted the family seven years later, Rose Lee was left to support three children—Jacob, 3-year-old

---

1. **sharecropper** (SHAIR-krahpuhr) *n.* a farmer who works the landowner's farm for a share of the crops

Geraldine, and 1-year-old William. In order to meet her family's needs, Rose Lawrence had to leave her children with foster parents while she worked as a domestic.[2]

Lawrence was 13 years old when Rose Lee Lawrence reunited with her children and moved the family to Harlem, in New York City. At that time, Harlem had the largest population of African Americans in the United States. It was also the most important cultural center for African Americans in the country.

Lawrence arrived in Harlem in 1930, at the end of an exciting era for African American artists, writers, and musicians. That time was known as the Harlem Renaissance. (See **Did You Know?** on page 92 for more information on the Harlem Renaissance.)

Fearing that he might get into trouble with neighborhood gangs, Jacob's mother enrolled him in a free after-school art class. It was a move she would soon regret. Young Jacob was so taken with painting that it was all he would do. "Every child paints. I just never stopped," Lawrence says.

Lawrence's mother tried to discourage her son from spending so much time painting and visiting New York City's art museums. She felt that he should prepare to become a civil servant.[3] Working for the post office provided a secure living for many young African American men at that time. "Blacks didn't think of going into fields like art or architecture because they knew that nobody would hire them," Lawrence recalls.

Lawrence continued to paint, however, and finally found someone who believed in his talent. Painter Charles Alston, an important artist of the Harlem Renaissance, became Jacob's first formal teacher. Lawrence also taught himself. He walked more than 60 blocks to spend hours at the Metropolitan Museum of Art, studying the styles and techniques of several artists. He particularly enjoyed the work of socially conscious[4] artists such as

---

2. **domestic** (duh-MEHS-tihk) *n.* a household servant
3. **civil servant** (SIH-vuhl SUHR-vuhnt) a person who works as a government employee
4. **conscious** (KAHN-shuhs) *adj.* being aware; concerned

Jan Brueghel (BROO-guhl), a Flemish painter who produced lively scenes of everyday life in the 16th century, and Francisco Goya, a Spanish painter whose art features brilliant, dramatic colors. Lawrence would then go home and use what he learned, by painting the activity and bright colors he saw in his home and community.

He also spent time at the studio of Augusta Savage, an African American artist who had studied and exhibited in Europe. With Savage's encouragement, Lawrence applied for a job at the WPA (Works Progress Administration) Harlem Art Workshop.

The WPA, a federally-funded program created in 1935, during President Franklin D. Roosevelt's administration, created 8 1/2 million jobs. Its purpose was to help the country recover from the Great Depression. The program created jobs building streets, highways, bridges, and national parks. It also hired artists, actors, writers, and musicians to produce new cultural works. When Lawrence was hired by the WPA, he earned $23.86 a week, a respectable[5] sum of money during the 1930s. The 18-month job gave him an opportunity to continue to study with his mentor,[6] Charles Alston.

His interest in African and African American history led Lawrence to produce a series of paintings on Toussaint L'Ouverture (too-SAN loo-vair-TOOR), the enslaved African who led the Haitian Revolution in 1795. Lawrence's series on Harriet Tubman and Frederick Douglass also focused on historical themes.

Lawrence spent hours at the Schomburg Library in Harlem, reading and taking notes about the Great Migration. As he progressed, his paintings became influenced by the style of Mexican muralist painter Diego Rivera, whose art stirred people to social action. With the security of a WPA position, Lawrence was able to begin work on the *Migration of the Negro* series.

---

5. **respectable** (rih-SPEHK-tuh-buhl) *adj.* fairly large in size or amount; deserving esteem
6. **mentor** (MEHN-tawr) *n.* a trusted counselor or guide

The year 1941 was an eventful one for Lawrence. Augusta Savage introduced him to Gwendolyn Knight, a beautiful young artist from the island of Barbados. The couple fell in love and was married. That year, Lawrence completed his *Migration* series and sold it to the Downtown Gallery, a prestigious[7] New York art gallery. The paintings drew such raves[8] from critics and art lovers that the Museum of Modern Art and the Phillips Gallery each bid to buy the entire series. A compromise was reached when the paintings were divided equally between the two art giants. The success of the *Migration* series established Lawrence's position in the U.S. art world.

Today, Lawrence's works are in the collections of major museums, universities, corporations, and serious private collectors around the world. He is professor emeritus[9] of painting at the University of Washington. He and Gwendolyn both maintain studios in their home in Seattle. The couple has no children, but Lawrence has long considered his students to be his children.

For more than 50 years, Lawrence's optimism and pride in his cultural history have enabled him to paint the courage, hopes, and dreams of African Americans. As reflected in the *Migration* series, "There was conflict and struggle," says Lawrence. "But out of the struggle came a kind of power and even beauty. *And the migrants kept coming* is a refrain of triumph over adversity. If it rings true for you today, then it must still strike a chord in our American experience."

> *Did You Know? Between 1920 and 1930, Harlem, a section of New York City, had some of the most fashionable African American residential neighborhoods in the United States. Many people were educated and middle class. Harlem was also a magnet for*

---

7. **prestigious** (preh-STIHJ-uhs) *adj.* highly honored or respected
8. **raves** (RAYVZ) *n. pl.* favorable criticism
9. **emeritus** (ih-MEHR-uht-uhs) *adj.* holding an honorary title after retirement

the African American artists, writers, and musicians who were part of the Harlem Renaissance. Talented African Americans were inspired and encouraged to draw upon their experiences in the rural South and the crowded cities of the North. The outpourings of their expressions on paper, on canvas, and in music remain important to culture in the United States today. During that period, African Americans produced outstanding novels, volumes of poetry, plays, and works of art. Determined to overcome racial prejudice, these artists often portrayed the lives of African Americans and their struggles to survive.

AFTER YOU READ

EXPLORING YOUR RESPONSES

1. Lawrence says, "Every child paints. I just never stopped." Describe something you enjoy learning so much that it's hard for you to stop.

2. Lawrence's mother enrolled him in an art class after school to keep him out of trouble. What other constructive activities could a teenager engage in after school?

3. Lawrence's mother encouraged him to seek a secure job with the post office. What would you have advised him to do?

4. Charles Alston believed in Lawrence's talent. How important is it for someone to get support from others?

5. Lawrence's parents moved north to improve their life. How do you think a person could improve his or her life?

UNDERSTANDING WORDS IN CONTEXT

Read the following sentences from the biography. Think about what each underlined word means. In your notebook, write what the word means as it is used in the sentence.

1. She felt that he should prepare to become a civil servant. Working for the post office provided a secure living for many young African American men at that time.

2. He particularly enjoyed the work of socially conscious artists such as Jan Brueghel, a Flemish painter who produced lively scenes of everyday life in the 16th century.

3. When Lawrence was hired by the WPA, he earned $23.86 a week, a respectable sum of money during the 1930s.

4. The 18-month job gave [Lawrence] an opportunity to continue to study with his mentor, Charles Alston.

5. That year, Lawrence completed his *Migration* series and sold it to the Downtown Gallery, a <u>prestigious</u> New York art gallery.

RECALLING DETAILS

1. How did art lessons change Lawrence's life?
2. Why did Lawrence's mother discourage him from painting?
3. Why was Charles Alston important to Lawrence?
4. How did the Works Progress Administration help people during the Depression?
5. What subjects does Lawrence paint?

UNDERSTANDING INFERENCES

In your notebook, write two or three sentences from the biography that support each of the following inferences.

1. Lawrence's early years were sometimes difficult.
2. Living in an important cultural center like Harlem inspired Lawrence to become an artist.
3. The great migration of African Americans that took place in the early 1900s influenced Lawrence's life.
4. The paintings Lawrence has created show what life has been like for African Americans.
5. Lawrence tries to be a mentor to developing artists.

INTERPRETING WHAT YOU HAVE READ

1. Why do you think some people cry when they see Lawrence's paintings?
2. Why do you think the Harlem Renaissance had such a strong influence on Lawrence?
3. How was Lawrence's life affected by prejudice?
4. How did Lawrence's museum visits influence his work?

5. Why do you think Lawrence chose to paint Toussaint L'Ouverture, Harriet Tubman, and Frederick Douglass?

ANALYZING QUOTATIONS

Read the following quotation from the biography and answer the questions below.

> For more than 50 years, Lawrence's optimism and pride in his cultural history have enabled him to paint the courage, hopes, and dreams of African Americans.

1. What does this quote tell you about how Lawrence feels about his African American heritage?
2. What does it mean to have "optimism and pride in your cultural history"?
3. How could you express pride in your own heritage?

THINKING CRITICALLY

1. Look at the photograph of Lawrence's work on page 88. Describe the painting and your response to it.
2. Why do you think Lawrence chose to be a painter?
3. In what ways might Lawrence's life have been different if he had gone to work for the post office?
4. How important is it to choose work that you enjoy?
5. Many people helped Lawrence throughout his career. How has someone helped you achieve a goal?

LORNA SIMPSON

Lorna Simpson doesn't want her photographs to simply record everyday experiences. She wants them to make people stop and think—about art and about African American concerns. Simpson's work has been featured in many galleries, including the Museum of Modern Art in New York City.

The images are of an African American woman. They show her body from just above her lips to just below the neckline of her white dress. "Ring, surround, lasso, noose," read the labels on the work. Underneath, in red, is the phrase "feel the ground sliding from under you." For African Americans who view the work, there is a flood of emotions connected with slavery, fear, and anger. Whites might feel shame or sympathy. They might also feel angry. No one is left untouched by Lorna Simpson's work.

Simpson is one of the most provocative[1]—and successful—African American artists working today. Her stark[2] black-and-white photographs with their simple labels demand attention. They demand that the viewer see with new eyes.

Lorna Simpson has been thinking about art and its meaning for people for most of her life. She was born in Crown Heights, Brooklyn, New York, in 1960. Hers was a middle-class family. Her mother, Eleanor, was a medical secretary. Her father, Elian, was a social worker. The dinner table was a place to discuss the problems of the world. "We'd talk about all the things with the civil rights issues that were going on in the '60s," her mother Eleanor says, "things that you have to tell your children about."

Simpson, who is an only child, was "interested in artistic things, but she never said to me she was going to be an artist," her mother says. Simpson took art, ballet, and violin lessons. "Gradually, she went to museums and things, and she got more and more interested" in art, her mother says. Simpson's parents also took her to concerts and Broadway plays.

Simpson was admitted to the High School of Art and Design, a competitive high school in New York City. She graduated from

1. **provocative** (pruh-VAHK-uht-ihv) *adj.* intending to excite or provoke
2. **stark** (STAHRK) *adj.* plain; without ornament

that school in 1978. Then she enrolled in the School of Visual Arts, a college for artists, in New York City. She painted, but "I wasn't a very good painter," she says. "I would spend weeks locked in painting, painting, and my friends would go zip, zip, zip, and make a fierce painting." But when she took a photography course, Simpson found her focus.

At college she became interested in African American artists, but she found no help in learning about them. "I realized that very little was said about artists of color," she says. To learn more, she did an internship[3] at the Studio Museum of Harlem to meet African American artists. She graduated from the School of Visual Arts in 1982. Then she explored documentary[4] photography, taking pictures of street life in Europe, Africa, and New York City. In many ways, Simpson's work was following a long line of African American artists who worked in photography. (See *Did You Know?* on page 102 for more information on early African American photographers.)

Next, Simpson went to the University of California at San Diego to pursue her master's degree in fine arts. By then, she had become unhappy with the way people looked at her photographs. They saw what they wanted to see, she says. Simpson wanted to shake up those ways of seeing. She began to experiment with adding words to her images. By adding words, she found, she could help people look at images in an unexpected way.

She also began to take photographs of people from the neck down. "The viewer wants so much to see a face, to read 'the look in the eyes' or the expression on the mouth," she says. "I wanted viewers to realize that it is one of the mechanisms[5] which they use to read a photograph. If they think 'How am I supposed to read this, if I don't see the face?' they may be too

---

3. **internship** (IHN-tuhrn-shihp) *n.* a job, paid or unpaid, that allows a student to get experience working in a profession
4. **documentary** (dahk-yuh-MEHNT-uh-ree) *adj.* based on facts
5. **mechanisms** (MEHK-uh-nihz-uhmz) *n. pl.* processes; systems for doing something

limited in what they see. Also, without faces in a photograph," Simpson says, "you could place yourself in the picture."

By using these devices[6] in her art, Simpson can shape the way people look at her work. She can also help direct the questions they ask themselves. They can, for example, look at the photograph of a young African American woman's neck, read the word *noose*, and think about the relationship between the word and the image. They can imagine themselves in the picture.

At first, Simpson's approach was not appreciated by mainstream[7] art buyers and galleries. She exhibited most of her work in African American-owned galleries. "I never looked toward galleries or white institutions to support my work," she says. "I went through either individuals or institutions that had a much more pluralistic[8] sense of what they wanted to show." In 1986, she had her first solo exhibition at New York City's Just Above Midtown Gallery.

Two years later, after she had placed pieces in several shows in New York City and Boston, white gallery owner Josh Baer saw them and became interested in Simpson's work. He visited her in her studio and asked to carry her work in his popular gallery in New York. Showing Simpson's work has made the gallery more popular. "The response to the work was immediately explosive," Baer says. Simpson's first solo show in his gallery, in 1989, was a sellout. Today, Simpson is one of the few African Americans to be represented by a mainstream art gallery. Simpson continues her association with the African American galleries that first supported her, though.

In 1990, Simpson's horizons widened even more. She became the first African American woman to have her work at the Venice Biennale, one of the world's most important art shows. That year, she also had a one-woman, summer-long exhibit at the Museum of Modern Art's Painting and Sculpture Gallery in

---

6. **devices** (dih-VEYES-uhz) *n. pl.* techniques; methods to achieve an artistic result
7. **mainstream** (MAYN-streem) *adj.* related to the dominant culture
8. **pluralistic** (ploor-uh-LIHS-tihk) *adj.* having to do with different groups

New York City. It is an honor that few artists ever win. Simpson, who was 30 in 1990, achieved it at a very early age. That year, she was also the subject of a half-hour segment of the PBS program on the arts, "Edge."

As Simpson's star rises, she continues to challenge herself. "I work very unevenly," she says. "I need to be able to step back from a project to see if it makes any sense."

One recent work is displayed in old slave quarters in Charleston, South Carolina. She researched the site, and looked to her own family for inspiration. Among old family photographs, she found a picture of a woman from her mother's family that was taken right after the woman was freed. The work also includes photographs of the backs of African American women's heads connected by braids that could be chains—or family connections. The piece includes a recording of jazz singer Billie Holiday's "Strange Fruit." In this work, Simpson is commenting on slavery, and "my contemporary[9] connection to it," she says.

Another piece, called "Places with a Past," features large corked bottles that stand on four-legged stools. Some are as tall as a person. Others are waist-high. The bottles contain different amounts of water. Each bottle represents a ship that carried slaves to the United States. Each has a label. "Pear/Coast of Guinea," reads one. "Pear" refers to the name of a boat that carried enslaved people. "Coast of Guinea" is one of the ports from which the ships left Africa.

In some ways, her unusual art changes the way artists work. She does not want viewers to look at her art and see what they want to see. She wants to direct their reactions. "It would be pretty ambitious of me to think that my work is effecting political change, but I do think public art—and hopefully my art—makes people stop and think," Simpson says. If that is her aim, Simpson is right on target. Her art makes viewers stop and think. Then they go home and think again.

---

9. **contemporary** (kuhn-TEHM-puh-rehr-ee) *adj.* modern; having to do with today

Did You Know? *As early as the 1840s, African Americans had access to cameras. Some photographers established themselves as artists. Others took portraits of people's weddings and special events. Their works recorded what would become part of African American history. Photographs of day-to-day life in small rural towns and large cities, of young students in classrooms, of laborers in steel mills, of small celebrations like picnics or weddings, and of important events that drew thousands all offer images of the African American experience from long ago. Portraits of famous African Americans, such as Harriet Tubman, leader of the Underground Railroad; freedom fighter Frederick Douglass; and educator Booker T. Washington often reveal more about their character than words. One of the largest collections of photographs by African Americans taken from 1840 through 1940 can be found in the New York Public Library's Schomburg Center for Research in Black Culture.*

EXPLORING YOUR RESPONSES

1. If you could choose a form of art to express your ideas, which would you choose? Why?

2. Lorna Simpson went out of her way to find out about African American artists. Do you think it is important for people to learn about successful people from their cultural group? Why or why not?

3. Simpson used her internship to study African American artists. If you could study one subject in depth, what would it be? Explain your choice.

4. Lorna Simpson likes art that helps people see things in new ways. Describe a photograph or painting that helped you to see something differently.

5. Think about a piece of art—visual, musical, or other—that has touched you. Explain your response.

UNDERSTANDING WORDS IN CONTEXT

Read the following sentences from the biography. Think about what each underlined word means. In your notebook, write what the word means as it is used in the sentence.

1. Her stark black-and-white photographs with their simple labels demand attention.

2. To learn more, she did an internship at the Studio Museum of Harlem to meet African American artists.

3. She graduated from the School of Visual Arts in 1982. Then she explored documentary photography, taking pictures of street life in Europe, Africa, and New York City.

4. By using these devices in her art, Simpson can help shape the way people look at her work.

5. At first, Simpson's approach was not appreciated by <u>mainstream</u> art buyers and galleries. She exhibited most of her work in African American-owned galleries.

RECALLING DETAILS

1. Describe Simpson's childhood.

2. Why did Simpson do an internship with the Studio Museum of Harlem?

3. Why was Simpson unhappy with the way people looked at her photographs?

4. Why did Simpson start photographing people without including their faces?

5. Why does Simpson put labels with her photographs?

UNDERSTANDING INFERENCES

In your notebook, write two or three sentences from the biography that support each of the following inferences.

1. Simpson wants people who see her work to have strong emotions about it.

2. Simpson feels that people view photographs in predictable ways.

3. Simpson thinks that faces in photographs can mislead the viewer.

4. Simpson finds inspiration for her work in her culture.

5. Simpson wants to change people's ideas.

INTERPRETING WHAT YOU HAVE READ

1. How do you think the label "Ring, surround, lasso, noose" relates to Simpson's photographs of African American women's necks?

2. How do you think Simpson's childhood influenced her choice of career?

3. How do you think being African American influences Simpson's art?

4. Why do you think Simpson felt at home with photography rather than painting?

5. Why does Simpson include words in her work?

ANALYZING QUOTATIONS

Read the following quotation from the biography and answer the questions below.

> *"It would be pretty ambitious of me to think that my work is effecting political change, but I do think public art—and hopefully my art—makes people stop and think."*

1. Why does Simpson hope people "stop and think" when they see her art?

2. What does this quotation tell you about Simpson's reason for creating art?

3. What are some ways that people might cause political change?

THINKING CRITICALLY

1. How might Simpson's life have been different if she had been raised in a poor family?

2. What do you think Simpson learned during her internship with the Studio Museum of Harlem?

3. Why did Simpson want people to "place themselves in the picture" when they looked at her photographs?

4. What is Simpson's "contemporary connection" to slavery?

5. If you wanted to make people look at ordinary things in a new way, how would you do it?

BRANFORD and WYNTON MARSALIS

Branford (left, on saxophone) and Wynton Marsalis (right, on trumpet) perform. The two brothers lead bands—Branford on "The Tonight Show with Jay Leno," and Wynton at Lincoln Center. They have also earned many Grammy awards, and the respect of musicians and fans in the fields of classical, jazz, and rock music.

Some people confuse Branford Marsalis with his brother Wynton. That isn't surprising, since these brothers were born only 14 months apart. Branford was born in August 1960; Wynton, in October 1961. They are both handsome and young. In addition, they are two of the most famous jazz musicians in the world.

Branford leads the band on "The Tonight Show with Jay Leno." Wynton is the jazz director at Lincoln Center in New York. Many critics credit them with renewing interest in jazz in the United States. Fans describe them as "cool." (See **Did You Know?** on page 112 for more information about the origins of jazz.)

Although Branford works in a television studio on the West Coast, and Wynton is based on the East Coast, their job responsibilities are similar. Both are leaders and spokesmen for their musical groups. They are also responsible for deciding who will play with their groups, which selections the groups will play, and which guest artists will perform with them. But, while the brothers resemble one another and have similar jobs and interests, their personalities are quite different.

Wynton, who plays the trumpet, tends to be more reserved.[1] He is famous for his contributions to classical music as well as jazz. Thus, he commands respect from classical music buffs who may have once believed that jazz is not a "serious" art form.

---

1. **reserved** (rih-ZERVD) *adj.* quiet in speech and manner; self-restrained

Proof of Wynton's success is the establishment of his 19-member jazz orchestra at Lincoln Center, a bastion[2] of classical music. He was also the first artist to win classical and jazz Grammy awards in the same year, 1984. He repeated this feat in 1985. To date, he has won eight Grammys.

Big brother Branford, who plays the saxophone, is usually the one with the smile and the sharp retort.[3] When a reporter asked him if he thought he had been picked to lead the band on Jay Leno's show because he is African American, Branford responded that he first turned the show's producers down. He noted that several white performers were considered before producers made the offer the second time. He added, "I don't think they sat around and figured, 'Let's get a list of Negroes and find out which one will do it.'" When asked if he felt that he was lucky to be offered this position, Branford said, "Our band plays well, so we've earned the right to be there. It was good fortune Jay called us. I create my own fortune, in a way. These opportunities come, I take advantage of them. I think of myself as charmed."

Both brothers can be seen in the most elegant of designer suits. But it was Branford who once appeared on "The Tonight Show" in a bikini. Branford has a second career as well, in acting. He has appeared in Danny DeVito's *Throw Mama From the Train* and Spike Lee's *School Daze*.

Wynton does not feel that his talents will take him in that direction. He says of acting, "I wouldn't disrespect that medium[4] by trying to be a part of it." Loving something, Wynton reasons, does not mean you are good at it. "I'd love to paint, but when I look at what I've done, I feel sorry for the canvas."

Wynton's serious personality is reflected in his choice of a favorite musician. When he was asked to name the greatest Western musician, he pointed to the 18th-century German

---

2. **bastion** (BAS-chuhn) *n.* a stronghold
3. **retort** (rih-TAWRT) *n.* a quick, witty reply
4. **medium** (MEE-dee-uhm) *n.* a means of communicating to the general public, such as newspapers, radio, TV, and movies

composer, Johann Sebastian Bach. "You can't get any higher than Bach. . . ." As for rap music, he describes it as "someone cursing over a beat."

Branford disagrees. Like his brother, he is respected in both jazz and classical music. But he says rap has "really artistic elements." He played with the rap group Public Enemy on their recording "Fight the Power." He has also played with Tina Turner, Shanice, Bruce Springsteen, and Sting. Branford's performances with Sting annoyed Wynton. He felt that his big brother should concentrate on the orchestral music he had been trained to play. Wynton spoke out publicly about his disappointment in Branford's decision. This occurred in 1985. This disagreement was painful, but the brothers have since reconciled.[5]

Wynton was not the only person to condemn Branford for playing with rock musicians. "People said I sold out to play with Sting," says Branford. "That's a value judgment that has little to do with how well a guy plays. . . . [Sting] can take different styles of music and incorporate them into his own, which is kind of what we do as jazz musicians."

Sometimes it is hard to believe that they come from the same family. Born in New Orleans, they have four other brothers. Their father, Ellis Marsalis, is a highly respected jazz pianist and music educator. Their mother, Dolores Marsalis, was a jazz singer and a substitute teacher before she became a full-time homemaker. She encouraged her sons to explore different areas in the arts. She gave the boys lots of books to read, and took them to music camps and classical music concerts, even though she did not enjoy classical music.

At home, the brothers enjoyed a healthy competitiveness. During a dinner of a favorite dish, such as fried shrimp, they worked hard at getting the last piece. Branford recalls making up an argument to divert[6] his younger brother's attention from the dinner table. By the time Wynton turned back to the shrimp

---

5. **reconciled** (REHK-uhn-seyeld) *v.* became friendly again; brought into harmony
6. **divert** (duh-VERT) *v.* to distract someone

platter, Branford had taken the last shrimp. Then, if Wynton complained, Branford would strike an innocent pose and ask, "What's he talking about?"

Jokes aside, Branford was playing clarinet and piano by the time he reached the second grade. At 15, he took up the alto saxophone because his father said it was the hardest sax to play. Wynton was given a trumpet when he was 6, but he was more interested in basketball and the Boy Scouts than he was in making music. Wynton recalls, "When I was 12, I thought it was cool to hang out on the street. I was trying to pursue an ignorant agenda,[7] like stealing, fighting."

Once, Wynton and a buddy almost set fire to a house that was being built. His mother heard about it and bitterly scolded him in front of his friends. From then on, she insisted he remain home when school was out so that she could keep an eye on him. "It blew my cool in the neighborhood. . . . She cured me of wanting to hang out on the streets."

Confined to the house, Wynton began to develop his interest in music, and to make up for the time he had lost. When Wynton was 15, he and Branford formed a funk-rock band called The Creators. Branford says, "The idea was to be funky and we could never quite cut it." Branford had been listening to Led Zeppelin, Aretha Franklin, Elton John, and Parliament-Funkadelic. He wanted to play the electric guitar, but his father would not allow it.

After graduating from high school in 1978, Branford entered Southern University in Baton Rouge, Louisiana. He did so well in his classical music studies that one of his teachers persuaded him to transfer to the Berklee College of Music, a highly respected school located in Boston, Massachusetts.

Since his mother's public scolding, Wynton had developed a more serious outlook. He used every free moment to practice or to listen to countless recordings that featured the trumpet. Just as his brother had before him, Wynton won many local music

---

7. **agenda** (uh-JEHN-duh) *n.* a list or plan of things to do

honors. When he was 17, a famous music center in Tanglewood, Massachusetts, waived the 18-year-old age requirement to allow him to attend. Wynton says, "I knew they couldn't believe that a 17-year-old who could play classical music also knew a lot about jazz."

In spite of Wynton's devotion to practice, he maintained a 3.98 average (on a scale of 4.0) and was a National Merit Scholarship finalist. Yale University offered him a scholarship, but he decided to attend the Juilliard School of Music in New York City instead.

Wynton was at Juilliard for two years. Then, in 1981, he began to accept offers to work with a variety of famous jazz bands. By this time, Branford had left school and was also making a name for himself in the music world. However, Wynton preceded[8] his older brother to fame. He won his first "double" Grammy in 1984.

The brothers, with their father, have made recordings together. They are known as the first family of jazz. Wynton has changed his mind about the need to focus on only one style of music. He no longer feels that Branford should have refused to play with Sting. "I used to think that was all a waste of time, but I now realize that different types of music have different functions."

Now that they are adults, they have children of their own. Branford has one son; Wynton has two. Wynton lives in Brooklyn, New York; Branford lives outside Los Angeles, California. Though they are separated by many miles, they share something important. They believe that hard work is the key to success. They preach this message as they lead student workshops at public schools around the country.

Says Wynton, "Kids always ask, 'How were you discovered?' and I say, 'Man, when *I* discovered the practice room.' You won't get anywhere without sweat." They are two brothers who enjoy working up a sweat while they keep cool.

---

8. **preceded** (prih-SEED-uhd) *v.* went before

Did You Know? *Jazz originated in the United States. Its roots date back to the first Africans who arrived on U.S. soil. They came with memories of the music they had heard and played in their native countries. The earliest African American music form was the work songs that slaves sang as they labored. Later, as their lives were shaped by Christianity, slaves began to sing gospel and spiritual music. From their weddings and other celebrations grew the ragtime dance music of the 19th century. Jazz is influenced by all these African American musical traditions: the short, fast beats of dance music and the "singing" instrumental solos. Over the years, jazz has risen from an obscure art form to one of the most original and respected music styles of the 20th century.*

AFTER YOU READ

EXPLORING YOUR RESPONSES

1. Branford and Wynton are similar in many ways, but they are also quite different. Describe how two brothers or sisters you know are similar, and how they are different.

2. Wynton and Branford had different views on rap music. How would you describe rap music?

3. Wynton publicly criticized Branford for playing with Sting. Describe ways that people can resolve their differences.

4. The brothers competed when they were boys. Why do you think relatives or friends sometimes compete?

5. Wynton was scolded in front of his friends for his misbehavior. Was his mother right to do this? Explain.

UNDERSTANDING WORDS IN CONTEXT

Read the following sentences from the biography. Think about what the underlined words mean. In your notebook, write what the word means as it is used in the sentence.

1. Big brother Branford, who plays the saxophone, is usually the one with the smile and the sharp retort.

2. He says of acting, "I wouldn't disrespect that medium by trying to be a part of it."

3. This disagreement was painful, but the brothers have since reconciled.

4. Branford recalls making up an argument to divert his younger brother's attention from the dinner table.

5. "I was trying to pursue an ignorant agenda, like stealing, fighting."

RECALLING DETAILS

1. Describe the differences between the personalities of Branford and Wynton.

2. How are their jobs similar?

3. What do Branford and Wynton think about forms of music other than jazz?

4. How did Dolores Marsalis influence her sons' careers?

5. What do both brothers believe is the key to success?

UNDERSTANDING INFERENCES

In your notebook, write two or three sentences from the biography that support each of the following statements.

1. Wynton's mother worried about his behavior.

2. Branford is not afraid of taking risks.

3. People can disagree, yet respect one another.

4. Wynton changed the attitudes some classical music fans had about jazz.

5. Success depends on practice and hard work, not just luck.

INTERPRETING WHAT YOU HAVE READ

1. Why do you think the producers selected Branford to lead the band on "The Tonight Show with Jay Leno"?

2. Why do you think Branford chose to play the alto saxophone?

3. Why do you think Ellis Marsalis did not allow Branford to play the electric guitar?

4. Wynton criticized his brother for playing with a rock musician. Why do you think people "look down" on some forms of music?

5. What personality trait helped both brothers become successful? Explain.

ANALYZING QUOTATIONS

Read the following quotation from the biography and answer the questions below.

> *Says Wynton, "Kids always ask, 'How were you discovered?' and I say, 'Man, when I discovered the practice room.' You won't get anywhere without sweat."*

1. What did Wynton mean by "discovering" the practice room?

2. How important do you think it is for a performer to be "discovered"?

3. Which musician or musical group do you most admire? Explain your choice.

THINKING CRITICALLY

1. Dolores Marsalis took her sons to classical music concerts even though she did not enjoy the concerts. How involved should a parent become in a child's career choice?

2. Wynton says that when he was 12, "I was trying to pursue an ignorant agenda, like stealing, fighting." Do you agree that this is "ignorant" behavior? Explain.

3. Do you think it would be disrespectful for a person to take advantage of fame and accept a position in another field? Explain your answer.

4. One brother leads a jazz orchestra at Lincoln Center, and the other leads a band on a popular TV show. Which job might you enjoy more? Why?

5. Which brother would you enjoy meeting? Why?

CULTURAL CONNECTIONS

Thinking About What People Do

1. With a partner, prepare a radio interview in which one of you is the interviewer and the other is one of the artists in this unit. The interview should reveal as much as possible about the subject, including how the person achieved success. You may use quotes from the biography as part of the interview. Present your radio program to the class.

2. Imagine that you went to elementary school with one of the people in this unit. Write a letter to your former classmate in which you give the person support and encouragement in his or her career.

3. Select one of the people in the unit who you think made good career decisions. List the decisions and write two paragraphs describing how that person's life might have been different if he or she had made other choices.

Thinking About Culture

1. The section titled *Did You Know?* that follows each biography tells you about the subject's cultural history. Choose one of the people in the unit and explain how that information helps you understand him or her better.

2. Compare the ways in which the cultural heritage of two of the people in this unit affects their work.

3. In what ways can a person's cultural heritage be an advantage? Give examples from people's lives you know about, or from the biographies in this unit.

Building Research Skills

Work with a partner to complete the following activity.

Choose one of the people discussed in this unit whose art interests you. Then imagine that you have decided to do the same kind of work yourself. Make a list of questions you have about how to succeed in that field. You might begin with the following questions:

Hint: The Bibliography at the back of this book lists articles and books to help you begin your research.

☆ What kinds of skills and talent do I need for this work?

☆ How would I develop good skills in this art field?

☆ How long might it take to develop these skills?

Hint: Look in your library for videos and cassette tapes of concerts, dance, and theatrical productions.

☆ What sacrifices might I have to make to succeed?

☆ What income could I expect?

☆ Who would be a good teacher or advisor in this field?

Hint: You might want to talk to an art or dance instructor for more information about their fields.

Next, use resources in the library to find the answers to your questions. You may wish to develop a chart with the following headings.

Hint: See if your library lends copies of paintings and photographs.

Type of art career:
Skills/talents:
Type of training required:
Number of years of preparation:

Complete the chart, and write several paragraphs about the field you have researched. Create a classroom Career Portfolio that focuses on the work you and your classmates have selected.

Extending Your Studies

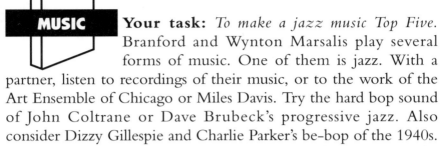

MUSIC **Your task:** *To make a jazz music Top Five.* Branford and Wynton Marsalis play several forms of music. One of them is jazz. With a partner, listen to recordings of their music, or to the work of the Art Ensemble of Chicago or Miles Davis. Try the hard bop sound of John Coltrane or Dave Brubeck's progressive jazz. Also consider Dizzy Gillespie and Charlie Parker's be-bop of the 1940s.

Before you listen, make sure you have a pencil and paper, and a comfortable place to sit. As you listen, let yourself doodle. Jazz music often brings out emotions in people. Do your doodles show how you feel? Do they seem soft and relaxed, or are they sharp and pointed? Compare doodles with your partner, and discuss how they are similar and different. How did you each respond to the same piece of music?

As a class, discuss your reactions to the pieces of jazz you have chosen. Make a list of Top Five Jazz Pieces to post for other students in your school.

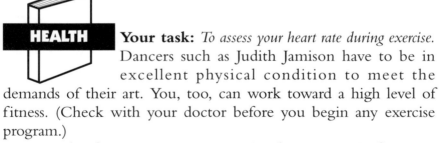

HEALTH **Your task:** *To assess your heart rate during exercise.* Dancers such as Judith Jamison have to be in excellent physical condition to meet the demands of their art. You, too, can work toward a high level of fitness. (Check with your doctor before you begin any exercise program.)

Begin by figuring out your resting heart rate. Before you exercise, place your fingers on the side of your neck, below your jaw, and count the number of pulse beats for ten seconds. Your count should begin with zero. Multiply this number by six to find your resting heart rate.

Now figure out your heart rate during exercise. To do this, choose an aerobic exercise (walking quickly, jogging, dancing, or bicycling) and do it for at least 15 minutes. Immediately take your pulse for 10 seconds. (Again, place your fingers on the side of your neck and count the pulse beats.) Multiply this number by six to figure out your exercising pulse rate.

Next, determine the percentage of maximum heart rate you are using. Your maximum heart rate is the number of times your heart beats each minute when you are exercising as hard as you can. Your maximum heart rate equals 220 minus your age. (For example, at 13 years old, a person's maximum heart rate is 207.)

Finally, divide your exercising pulse rate by your maximum heart rate to determine the percentage of your heart rate that you are using. To improve your level of fitness, you should reach 70 percent of your maximum heart rate each time you exercise.

When you finish exercising, walk slowly for ten minutes before checking your pulse rate again. Continue walking and cooling down until your pulse returns to its resting rate.

VISUAL ARTS **Your task:** *To create a collage that carries a message.* In this unit, you read about Jacob Lawrence's series of paintings titled *The Migration of the Negro*. The paintings carry a strong message. Some viewers were even brought to tears.

Create a collage that expresses powerful emotions. A collage is a work of art that may include pictures, news headlines, or found objects, including coins, sticks, rope, bottle caps, or other items.

Select one strong feeling to convey to your audience. Choose one from the following list, or use any other powerful emotion:

☆ love   ☆ hope

☆ fear   ☆ sorrow

☆ joy

Include in your collage items that will convey your message. Then title your collage, and display it in the classroom.

WRITING WORKSHOP

As you know, a biography is the true story of a person's life. In this lesson, you will write a **biographical sketch of someone you know**—a friend or classmate your own age. Since your biography will be a "sketch" of the person you choose, do not try to cover the person's entire life. Just think about an event or a situation that shows what this person is like. Then write your sketch to introduce your subject to the class.

PREWRITING

Begin your **prewriting** activities by selecting a classmate or friend whom you know well, and with whom you have shared some experience. Before you make your decision, though, review what you know about the person and the details of the experience you shared. Think about what happened, and what both of you did and said. Make sure you have a clear picture of the person and experience, so that you will be able to make the scene come alive for your reader. You might want to choose two or three possible subjects, then narrow your search.

Before you select one subject, decide which person and experience you remember best, and which you can describe best for your reader. Once you are sure of your subject and the experience you will discuss, you can continue your prewriting activities. Here are two suggestions:

Brainstorming: You may know which person and event you want to write about, but be unsure of how to begin. Brainstorming is one way to explore your topic. Think about your subject, and on a blank sheet of paper write any word or phrase that comes to mind. Try to use words that describe the person's character, appearance, habits, hobbies, and sense of humor. Use details that appeal to the senses.

As you brainstorm, include ideas or events that concern your subject. Think about how you know the person, for example, or when and where you met. Your brainstorming notes may look something like this:

Katie

my best friend	likes roller-blading
same age as I am	afraid of dogs
very tall and willowy	likes playing the piano
always joking	a big, loud laugh
lives in the city	can draw well
freckles	mischievous grin

Freewriting: Look at the words and ideas you brainstormed. Choose one that seems to jump out at you, and begin writing. Do not think too much about what you write; just write freely for two minutes. Your freewriting will help you create a word sketch of your subject.

Organize: Think about how you can use your brainstorming notes and the ideas or event you explored in your freewriting. Arrange your ideas so that they show the real person—what he or she is like as a person, not just his or her outward appearance.

DRAFTING

Now you can begin **drafting** your biographical sketch. Use the following strategies to help you begin:

Use specific language: Choose words that help your reader see and understand your subject. For example, read the following sentences. Which one gives you a clear picture of Katie?

Katie has a nice laugh.
Katie's rollicking laughter fills the whole room.

What do you know about Katie after you read both sentences? A "nice laugh" does not give you much detail, so it is difficult to get a strong impression of Katie. A "rollicking" laugh that "fills the whole room," though, probably makes you think of a very happy person with a loud, jolly laugh that makes everyone laugh with her. The second sentence, then, gives you enough detail to allow you to construct a mental picture of Katie.

As you draft your biographical sketch, use as much specific language as you can so that your reader can "see" your subject.

Now you are ready to write your draft. At this point, do not worry about word usage and spelling errors. Concentrate on getting your ideas down on paper in a clear, understandable way. You will check for errors when you proofread your work.

REVISING

Put your sketch aside for a day or two. Then, with the help of another student who will act as your editor, evaluate and **revise** your work. See the directions for writers and student editors below.

Directions for Writers: Read your work aloud, listening to how it flows. Then ask yourself these questions:

☆ Does my opening hold the reader's attention?

☆ Am I *showing,* not *telling,* what happened?

☆ Did I include interesting details?

☆ Does my description make my subject come alive?

Make notes for your next draft or revise your work before you give it to a student editor. Then ask your editor to read your work. Listen carefully to his or her suggestions. If they seem helpful, use them to improve your writing when you revise your work.

Directions for Student Editors: Read the work carefully and respectfully, remembering that your purpose is to help the writer do his or her best work. Keep in mind that an editor should always make positive, helpful comments that point to specific parts of the essay. After you read the work, use the following questions to help you direct your comments:

☆ What do I like most about this biographical sketch?

☆ Can I see the person or event in my mind?

☆ Do I feel I know the subject?

☆ Has the writer used details to describe the subject?

☆ What did the writer learn about his or her subject?

PROOFREADING

When you are satisfied that your work says what you want it to say, **proofread** it for errors in spelling, punctuation, capitalization, and grammar. Also look for wordy phrases that can be replaced with one precise word. Use the chart below as a guide. Then make a neat, final copy of your autobiographical essay.

Wordy Phrase	Precise Word
in order to	to
of a special kind	special
together with	with
of importance	important
by means of	by
small in size	small

PUBLISHING

After you have revised your writing, you are ready to **publish** or share it. Put together a classroom portrait gallery called Someone You Should Know, and display the sketches for everyone to read.

AFRICAN AMERICANS IN THE SCIENCES AND MATHEMATICS

In this unit you will read about five African Americans who have left their mark in the sciences and mathematics. As you read, think about some of the personal qualities they share, such as curiosity and a desire to do their best. Think, too, about what makes each person special.

Neurosurgeon **Benjamin Carson** believes that knowledge is the key to success. As he says, "You become valuable because of the knowledge that you have. And that doesn't mean you won't fail sometimes. The important thing is to keep trying."

Astronaut **Mae Jemison** believes in being the best she can be. She says, "I think too many folks are too busy telling children they can't do this or they can't do that. It's important that we start recognizing that every individual in society has skills and talents."

Biologist **Jewel Plummer Cobb** has the curiosity that is needed in a scientist. She tells of discovering the miniature world that can be seen through the lens of a microscope. "It was really awe-inspiring," she says. "Here's a world that I never even knew about!"

Computer engineer **Donna Auguste** found support at home. "In my family," she says, "people had great respect for differences."

Mathematician **Robert Moses** also believes that more of us can succeed. "What we're suffering from is a culture that says [that] to do well in math, you have to inherit genes from a parent who did well in math."

As you read the unit, think about how each person's curiosity and desire to meet challenges contributed to his or her choice of career.

BENJAMIN CARSON

Neurosurgeon Dr. Benjamin Carson examines images of a patient's brain. Carson's work gives his patients hope for their future. He also gives hope to students, telling them that they can make a difference by using their knowledge to help others.

The activity swirling around the operating room on September 5, 1987, resembled a military campaign. Five months of preparation had brought together a team of 70 doctors, nurses, and surgical assistants. An additional support staff of 70 people worked outside the room. Inside, 7-month-old twin boys, who had been born joined at the head, lay on the operating table.

At the center of this extraordinary event at Johns Hopkins Hospital in Baltimore, Maryland, was Dr. Benjamin S. Carson, who is one of only three African American chiefs of pediatric neurosurgery[1] in the United States.

Seventeen hours into the difficult procedure to separate the twins, the babies were bleeding profusely.[2] Fifty units of blood had already been used, and the hospital had no more of the correct type. If the team couldn't locate more blood, the babies would not survive. At the last minute, the American Red Cross found ten units of the desperately needed blood. (See **Did You Know?** on page 132 for more information about Dr. Charles Drew, an African American pioneer of blood banks.)

More than 22 hours after the operation began, the successful separation of the twins made international news. It also made a hero of the doctor who describes himself as a "ghetto kid from the streets of Detroit."

Ben Carson is the younger of two sons born to Sonya and Robert Carson in Detroit, Michigan, in 1951. He was 8 years old when his parents divorced. His mother was forced to rent out their small home and move to Boston with her sons, where they lived with relatives. During that year, Ben and his brother Curtis attended a private church school. Later, he realized that the school did not demand enough from him.

---

1. **neurosurgery** (NOŌR-oh-suhr-juh-ree) *n.* surgery on the brain or spinal cord
2. **profusely** (pruh-FYOOS-lee) *adv.* pouring forth in great quantities

At Christmas, Ben received a chemistry set. He spent hours studying the directions and then experimenting with chemical reactions. This was the beginning of a lifelong interest in science. It also led to his decision to become a doctor. Carson was captivated by the experiences of medical missionaries[3] in far-off lands described by his pastor. He felt that he wanted to become a medical missionary in Africa or India.

When the Carson family returned to Detroit, they moved to a new neighborhood. Sonya Carson supported her family by working as a domestic. The boys were enrolled in an elementary school in which most of the students were white. Carson, who had been a good student, was in for a shock. The classes were tough and "I was the worst student in my whole fifth grade," he recalls. Because he was at the bottom of the class in every subject, the other students teased him.

Carson's teacher had her students read their test scores aloud. For a few months, he endured this humiliation. He felt that being an African American with poor grades in a white class meant "having everything stacked against me." But two important things helped boost his self-esteem and change his life.

The first thing was the discovery that Carson's vision was poor. After he was given glasses, he was able to see the chalkboard and to read better.

The second thing was Sonya Carson's plan to make her son a better student. She had always had great faith in her sons' abilities. She would say, "I have two smart boys." But she was alarmed by Ben's midterm report card. She refused to let her son settle for failing grades.

Math was one of Carson's worst subjects. His mother told him that he was not to go outside and play after school until he had memorized his multiplication tables. "My tables?" Ben asked. "Do you know how many there are? Why, that could

---

3. **missionaries** (MIHSH-uhn-air-eez) *n. pl.* people who are sent to another culture to perform a special duty

take a year!" Sonya Carson reminded her son that she had only had a third-grade education. Yet she knew the multiplication tables all the way "through the twelves."

Carson worked at his multiplication tables. Soon his math grades began to soar. In fact, he rose to the top of his class. But Sonya Carson was determined to have her sons earn top grades in every class. She limited their TV viewing to three programs a week. The boys were expected to read at least two library books a week and to give their mother a report on what they'd read.

Carson wasn't too happy about this part of his mother's plan, which cut into his after-school fun. Yet he became fascinated with what he read in the science and nature books he borrowed. Soon he excelled in science, too. His interest in other topics grew. He also improved his vocabulary. By the end of the year, Carson was the top student in his entire fifth-grade class and had won the admiration of his classmates. He earned the highest grades in his class throughout junior high school. Every year, he won a special certificate of achievement that was given to the best student in each grade.

In the ninth grade, however, Carson was humiliated again. After he accepted his certificate of achievement and returned to his seat, a teacher scolded the students. She said that by letting Carson become the top student, they were not really trying. "While she never quite said it in words, she let them know that a black person shouldn't be number one in a class where everyone else was white," Carson says.

At the time, Carson was angry and determined to show the teacher, and anyone else who doubted him, that he deserved the award. He worked hard to keep up his grades, but he came to realize that he didn't want to simply compete with his classmates. He wanted to be the best for himself.

When it was time for Carson to go to college, he applied to Yale. With his excellent grades and high SAT scores, he was accepted and offered an academic scholarship that paid 90 percent of his expenses. During his freshman year, he was surrounded by bright, high-achieving students. The work was much more demanding than anything he'd done in high school. When he almost failed a chemistry exam, he realized that, once again, he had to change his study habits. He stopped wasting time during the semester, and then cramming[4] for his final exams. It was essential that he do well, especially in chemistry, because he wanted to study medicine.

After graduating from Yale, Carson went on to the University of Michigan. As a medical student, he rotated to a different medical field every month. During his month in neurosurgery, he knew that that was what he would do for the rest of his life. "The first few times I looked down upon a human brain, or saw human hands working upon the center of intelligence and emotion and motion, working to heal, I was hooked," he says.

After medical school, Carson served as an intern[5] at Johns Hopkins University Hospital. His professors and the nursing staff soon recognized that Carson was a talented surgeon. When a few patients protested that they didn't want an African American doctor, Dr. Long, his supervisor, calmly told them, "There's the door. You're welcome to walk through it. But if you stay here, Dr. Carson will handle your case."

In the spring of 1975, Ben Carson married Lacena Rustin, a gifted musician he had met at Yale. They had three sons. A few years later, he was invited to join the staff of Johns Hopkins University as a surgical resident.[6]

Most of Carson's patients have conditions such as brain tumors or severe head injuries that are disabling or life-threatening. Because his cases are often difficult to treat, he is always looking for ways to relieve his patients' suffering and restore them to health.

In 1985, as a professor of pediatric neurosurgery, Carson began to perform a surgical procedure known as a

---

4. **cramming** (KRAM-ihng) *v.* studying for an exam in a hurried, intensive way
5. **intern** (IHN-tuhrn) *n.* a doctor who is serving an apprenticeship as an assistant resident in a hospital
6. **resident** (REHZ-ih-duhnt) *n.* a person who is pursuing advanced medical or surgical training

hemispherectomy.[7] The procedure removes a hemisphere—or half—of the brain.

The operation is rarely performed because it is particularly risky. In fact, Carson says, "We can only do this operation on young children because their brain cells haven't decided what they want to do when they grow up." For example, if cells in a young child's body are injured or diseased, and must be removed by surgery, a set of cells on the other side of the brain can take over their task. While the operation is dangerous, many of his young patients are so seriously ill that by taking this risk, Carson believes, "there might be a whole world to gain" for them.

In 1985, a 4-year-old girl named Maranda was brought to Carson because she suffered from a rare form of epilepsy.[8] Maranda's body was shaken by more than 100 seizures a day. They weakened one side of her body and eventually prevented her from speaking or eating. The child's condition was so serious that Carson felt there was little choice but to perform the operation.

"I was going to do my best. And I went into the surgery with two things clear. First, if I didn't operate, Maranda . . . would worsen and die. Second, I had done everything to prepare myself for this surgery, and now I could leave the results in God's hands."

The operation was long and difficult, but Carson was successful. Maranda began to speak almost immediately after surgery. She was also able to eat, and move her weakened side again. Nine years later, she is a healthy child who takes tap-dancing lessons.

In 1990, Carson wrote a book titled *Gifted Hands*, which he dedicated to his mother. It is an inspiring book that tells in great detail how he learned to use his talents to help others.

Every month, Carson also takes time from his busy operating

7. **hemispherectomy** (hehm-uh-sfeer-EHK-tuh-mee) *n.* surgical removal of one half of the brain
8. **epilepsy** (EHP-uh-lehp-see) *n.* a physical disorder marked by convulsions

schedule to speak with students. After encouraging them to follow their dreams, he tells them that they don't have to become brain surgeons to be valuable people. "You become valuable because of the knowledge that you have. And that doesn't mean you won't fail sometimes. The important thing is to keep trying." Carson reminds his audiences that "Every hurdle we jump strengthens and prepares us for the next one, [and shows us that] we're already on the way to success."

> ***Did You Know?*** *At the beginning of World War II (1939-1945), there was a great demand for blood that could be used in transfusions. Such blood had to be stored for several weeks and be ready for use on the battlefield. Dr. Charles Richard Drew, an African American physician and medical researcher, and Dr. John Scudder demonstrated that using plasma could save lives during medical emergencies. Plasma is the liquid part of the blood. It contains no cells. Plasma can be stored longer than whole blood. It can also be given to people of all blood types without causing a dangerous reaction. In 1939, Drew became medical director of a Red Cross program that shipped plasma overseas. He developed a blood bank system that saved the lives of millions of servicemen and women, and civilians.*

AFTER YOU READ

EXPLORING YOUR RESPONSES

1. Carson reacted to his classmates' taunts by working harder. Why do you think young people tease one another?

2. Carson's career grew out of his interest in science. Do you think it is always a good idea to choose a career that interests you? Explain.

3. There were many times when Carson could have given up his goal to be a neurosurgeon. What do you think makes people strive for difficult goals?

4. Carson's mother forced him to study. Do young people sometimes need this discipline? Explain.

5. Many of the surgical operations Carson performs require taking risks. What factors do you consider before taking a risk?

UNDERSTANDING WORDS IN CONTEXT

Read the following sentences from the biography. Think about what each underlined word means. In your notebook, write what the word means as it is used in the sentence.

1. Seventeen hours into the difficult procedure to separate the twins, the babies were bleeding profusely.

2. Carson was captivated by the experiences of medical missionaries in far-off lands described by his pastor.

3. He stopped wasting time during the semester, and then cramming for his final exams.

4. After medical school, Carson served as an intern at Johns Hopkins University Hospital. His professors and the nursing staff soon recognized that Carson was a talented surgeon.

5. In 1985, a 4-year-old girl named Maranda was brought to Carson because she suffered from a rare form of epilepsy. Maranda's body was shaken by more than 100 seizures a day.

RECALLING DETAILS

1. What event began Carson's lifelong interest in science?
2. Why did Carson have difficulty in elementary school in Detroit?
3. How did Sonya Carson help her sons succeed in school?
4. How was Carson humiliated in ninth grade?
5. How did Carson react to this humiliation?

UNDERSTANDING INFERENCES

In your notebook, write two or three sentences from the biography that support each of the following inferences.

1. Sonya Carson provided the encouragement her sons did not receive in school.
2. At first, Carson competed with his classmates, but eventually he worked to challenge himself.
3. Carson enjoys being challenged.
4. Carson's job involves many risks.
5. Carson is proud of his background and heritage.

INTERPRETING WHAT YOU HAVE READ

1. Why do you think Carson describes himself as a "ghetto kid from the streets of Detroit"?
2. Why do you think Carson's experiences in elementary and high school had such a strong influence on him?
3. How do you think Carson's ideas about his mother's strict study plan changed when he was older?

4. How did Carson's motivation for working hard change as he got older?

5. Why do you think Carson encourages students to follow their dreams?

ANALYZING QUOTATIONS

Read the following quotation from the biography and answer the questions below.

> "You become valuable because of the knowledge that you have. And that doesn't mean you won't fail sometimes. The important thing is to keep trying."

1. How does knowledge make a person valuable?

2. What do you think makes people valuable?

3. How would you persuade a person to keep trying?

THINKING CRITICALLY

1. Do you think Sonya Carson was right to take such strong measures? Explain.

2. How did Carson's experiences in predominantly white schools affect his drive to succeed?

3. Do you agree or disagree that students should read their test scores aloud? Explain.

4. Why do you think Carson's teacher scolded the students for not trying hard enough?

5. What conclusions can you draw about the effects of prejudice?

MAE JEMISON

Physician and astronaut Mae Jemison sits in a Space Shuttle crew trainer at the Johnson Space Center in Houson, Texas. Jemison, who was the first African American astronaut, believes that people from all cultural groups should "reach for the stars."

The shuttle blasted off. From her seat hundreds of miles up in space, Mae Jemison, the first female African American astronaut, looked out at the slowly turning blue and green ball below. "The first thing I saw," says Jemison, "was Chicago," her hometown. Not long after, she saw Somalia, a country in Africa near where Jemison had worked as a doctor for the Peace Corps.

Those views of Earth from space reinforced[1] something Mae Jemison strongly believes. "Space belongs to all of us," she says. "I'm not the first or the only African American woman who had the skills and the talent to become an astronaut. I had the opportunity. All people have produced scientists and astronomers."

Jemison may have had the opportunity, but she also had something just as important. She had tenacity.[2] From the time Jemison was a small child, she was sure she would become an astronaut. "I recall looking up at the stars, wondering what was up there, knowing I'd go up there some day, although I didn't know how," she says.

When she was born, in 1956, astronauts were white men who flew jets for the military. Jemison paid no attention to that. Passion for space filled her childhood. When she was 10 to 14 years old, she says, she read astronomy books and began to visit Chicago's Museum of Science and Industry. Her teachers encouraged her, she says, letting her "go off and do things, explore on my own." She also credits her parents with always believing in their three children's abilities.

Jemison did well in school, and entered Stanford University in California on a National Achievement Scholarship when she was

1. **reinforced** (ree-uhn-FOHRST) *v.* strengthened
2. **tenacity** (tuh-NAS-uht-ee) *n.* the quality of holding fast; persistence

only 16. She remembers coming home for Christmas during her first year of college with her calculus book in hand. Her mother suggested that she ask her father, a roofer and carpenter, for help. "I thought she couldn't be serious," Jemison says. "My father is a high school graduate, and I was this, well, hotshot at Stanford. But I did ask him for help and he made it so clear to me. That one thing changed the way I thought about my father and myself."

Her mother, an elementary school teacher, also had a strong impact on Jemison's ideas. Jemison recalls telling her mother about an exciting science project she was involved with. Her mother answered that while she might know science, she didn't know much about other subjects. "I was crushed," Jemison says. She began to learn more about African American history and culture. When she graduated from Stanford, it was with degrees in chemical engineering, and African and African American studies. "Science is very important to me, but I also like to stress that you have to be well-rounded," she says. "I truly feel someone interested in science is interested in understanding what's going on in the world."

After graduation, she was accepted to Cornell University Medical College in Ithaca, New York. While she attended medical school there, she traveled to Cuba, Kenya, and Thailand, where she studied and worked as a volunteer. Jemison did not look on her work as charity. "I've gotten much more out of what I have done than the people I was supposed to be helping," she says.

After she earned her medical degree, she thought of trying to be an astronaut. She decided against this idea, though, because she felt that she had not had enough experiences. Then she joined the Peace Corps as a doctor in the African countries of Sierra Leone and Liberia. "At 26, I was one of the youngest doctors over there, and I had to learn to deal with how people reacted to my age while asserting[3] myself as a physician."

---

3. **asserting** (uh-SUHRT-ihng) *v.* stating one's position forcefully

After almost three years in the Peace Corps, Jemison returned to the United States in 1985 and took a job as a doctor with CIGNA, a health maintenance organization in Los Angeles. In 1986, she applied for a job with NASA, the National Aeronautics and Space Administration. Early the next year, Jemison got a call from Houston. "I didn't know anyone in Houston. It could have only been one thing." It was. Jemison had made it through the first round of 2,000 applicants.

In between intensive[4] medical tests, background checks, and interviews, Jemison continued her medical practice. In June of 1987, she received another call from Houston. Her childhood dream was becoming reality.

Making this dream come true meant years of hard work. After a rigorous[5] year-long training program, Jemison worked on the ground for NASA for five years, before her first mission in space. In September, 1992, she boarded the space shuttle *Endeavour* for an eight-day trip into outer space. "I had this big smile on my face," Jemison remembers. "I was so excited. This is what I had wanted to do for a very long time."

Although the *Challenger* shuttle disaster that killed seven astronauts had happened only years before, Jemison had no fear. "You are aware that you are sitting on a controlled explosion. But you also realize that you've taken all the precautions. You trust the people you have been working with, and you know they have worked to try to keep things safe. After that, you have to leave it alone."

One of her tasks on the *Endeavour* was to research what would happen to tadpoles in space. Frogs, like other living things, take clues for how they grow from their environment. Would tadpoles develop differently in the weightless world on board the spacecraft? The answer to that question could help answer other questions about what space travel might do to humans. The tadpoles, Jemison discovered, developed normally.

---

4. **intensive** (ihn–TEN–sihv) *adj.* highly concentrated
5. **rigorous** (RIHG–uh–ruhs) *adj.* very strict; demanding

Other investigations involved motion sickness in space, which had troubled many astronauts. The weightlessness of space can cause dizziness and illness. Jemison experimented with biofeedback, a way of using one's mind to control the responses of the body. She also studied the problem of astronauts losing calcium from their bones during long trips.

After her return from space, Jemison discovered she had become a celebrity. She took the chance to make her views heard, and to show that African American women have a place in exploring the universe. "People don't see women—particularly black women—in science and technology fields," she says.

She had to answer the criticism that African Americans should have no interest in space when there are so many pressing needs at home. Jemison has a ready answer. Although some may believe that space travel has only been the interest of wealthy, industrialized nations, she says, "this is not so. Ancient African empires—Mali, Songhai, Egypt—had scientists, astronomers. The fact is that space and its resources belong to all of us, not to any one group." And if Africans, and African Americans, are not in on the exploration, "helping to determine what happens to these resources, we'll have no say in how they are used," she says. "We need to get every group involved because it is something that eventually we in the world community are going to have to share." (See **Did You Know?** on page 141 for more information about ancient African astronomers.)

Jemison's achievements have earned her a shelf full of awards. She won the 1988 *Essence* Science and Technology Award, several honorary doctorates, the 1992 Ebony Black Achievement award, and she was named a Montgomery Fellow at Dartmouth College in 1993. In 1992, the Mae C. Jemison Academy, an alternative public school in Detroit, was named for her.

In 1993, she left NASA to begin her own company. The Jemison Group researches, markets, and develops advanced technologies. One of her projects uses satellite communications to improve health care in West Africa by allowing doctors and patients to communicate more quickly. By starting this company, Jemison is once again traveling in unknown territory. But she has never let anyone else's ideas of what was possible stop her. "I believe you should do things you want to do, regardless of whether anyone's been there before," she says.

Even though she tries to downplay her achievements, Jemison understands that for many young people she is a symbol of what African Americans and women can accomplish. Is she a role model? "That's for other people to decide," she says. "But I do think that I serve as an important image for society in general. Certainly for young black girls who need to see themselves represented in all spheres,[6] but just as much for older white males." Those men, she says, are often the ones who make the decisions, and if they see the achievements of people like Jemison, they may open opportunities to more African Americans and women.

"I think too many folks are too busy telling children they can't do this or they can't do that. It's important that we start recognizing that every individual in society has skills and talents. Let them use those talents." In encouraging others to follow their dreams, Mae Jemison continues to reach the stars.

> **Did You Know?** Since prehistoric times, people in Africa have studied the stars. The remains of an ancient observatory were found in Kenya. This observatory dates back to 300 years B.C. Huge stone pillars form a calendar which indicates the rising of the stars and the location of the constellations. The astronomer–priests of the Dogon people in Mali, a country in West Africa, have long understood details about the solar system that modern astronomers have only begun to detect.

---

6. **spheres** (SFIHRS) *n. pl.* areas

AFTER YOU READ

EXPLORING YOUR RESPONSES

1. If you were an astronaut looking down at Earth, what would you most want to see?

2. Jemison had the dream of becoming an astronaut when she was a child. Does being an astronaut sound exciting to you? Why or why not?

3. Do you think a person needs to know about many things to be good in a profession? Explain.

4. Jemison says people should do what they want "regardless of whether anyone's been there before." How could this attitude be helpful? How might it be troublesome?

5. Mae Jemison believes role models are important. Describe someone who is a role model to you or someone you know.

UNDERSTANDING WORDS IN CONTEXT

Read the following sentences from the biography. Think about what each underlined word means. In your notbook, write what the word means as it is used in the sentence.

1. Those views of Earth from space reinforced something Mae Jemison strongly believes. "Space belongs to all of us," she says.

2. "At 26, I was one of the youngest doctors over there, and I had to learn to deal with how people reacted to my age while asserting myself as a physician."

3. In between intensive medical tests, background checks, and interviews, Jemison continued her medical practice.

4. After a rigorous year-long training program, Jemison worked on the ground for NASA for five years, before her first mission in space.

5. "But I do think that I serve as an important image for society in general. Certainly for young black girls who need to see themselves represented in all spheres, but just as much for older white males."

RECALLING DETAILS

1. Trace the path of Jemison's career.

2. What research did Jemison conduct in space?

3. How were ancient Africans involved in space?

4. Why does Jemison think it is important to have African Americans in the space program?

5. What kind of work does The Jemison Group do?

UNDERSTANDING INFERENCES

In your notebook, write two or three sentences from the biography that support each of the following inferences.

1. Jemison's career focuses on helping others.

2. Jemison's parents influenced her view of the world.

3. Jemison does not feel limited by what other people think is possible.

4. Jemison puts herself in situations that will challenge her.

5. Jemison brings the viewpoint of an African American woman to the questions about how space should be explored.

INTERPRETING WHAT YOU HAVE READ

1. How did Jemison's personality help her become successful?

2. How do you think Jemison changed her thinking about her father, and the world, after he helped her with her calculus?

3. How do you think waiting to apply to NASA helped Jemison when she did become an astronaut?

4. Why do you think Jemison left NASA to start her own company?

5. How do you think Jemison would like the resources of space to be used?

ANALYZING QUOTATIONS

Read the following quotation from the biography and answer the questions below.

> *"Space belongs to all of us," she says. "I'm not the first or the only African American woman who had the skills and the talent to become an astronaut. I had the opportunity. All people have produced scientists and astronomers."*

1. What do you think Jemison means when she says, "Space belongs to all of us"?

2. What can you tell about Jemison from reading this quotation?

3. Why do you think Jemsion wants others to know that all people have produced scientists and astronomers?

THINKING CRITICALLY

1. How do you think Jemison was able to overcome obstacles to her success?

2. How do you think Jemison's time in Africa influenced her later life?

3. If you had been working for NASA and looking for astronauts, what about Mae Jemison would have attracted you?

4. How do you think Jemison feels about being celebrated as the first African American woman in space?

5. If you were a role model, and young people were paying attention to what you said, what lesson would you most want them to learn?

JEWEL PLUMMER COBB

DO NOT USE TOXIC, EXPLOSIVE, OR FLAMMABLE SUBSTANCES IN THIS CABINET

Biologist Jewel Plummer Cobb discovers new worlds through a microscope. Cobb, who has also been a college president, encourages African American students and women to discover the worlds available to them through careers in the sciences.

Jewel Plummer Cobb enjoyed the dinner table discussions she had with her father, Frank Plummer, who was a doctor. They talked about his cases, about medicine, about science. But Cobb always figured she would follow her mother Carriebel and become a dancer or a physical education teacher. Then, one day in high school, Cobb looked into a microscope and found another universe. Cobb was fascinated. "It was really awe-inspiring," she says. "Here's a world I never even knew about." Since then, it is a world she has never left.

Cobb's family has been involved with science for generations. Her grandfather graduated from historically black Howard University in 1898 as a pharmacist. Her father graduated from Cornell University, and earned his medical degree from Rush Medical School in Chicago in 1923, the year before Jewel was born.

Frank Plummer's practice mainly served the African Americans who had recently migrated to the North. He set up his office at a streetcar transfer point for stockyard workers, so that they could see him on the way to or from work.

Cobb's mother studied dancing and physical education at Sargeants, a college connected with Harvard University in Boston. She was a teacher of dance in the Chicago public schools.

The Plummer home was filled with books. Their friends—historians, producers of plays, writers—were well-known in Chicago's African American world. During the summers, the Cobbs left the hot city for Idle Wild, a resort in northern Michigan where many African American families had second homes.

Her family's position and money protected Cobb from many of the problems of African Americans. Cobb saw, however, how poorly most of her father's patients lived. She also learned, decades later, that Chicago kept most African Americans out of its schools by drawing boundaries[1] around traditionally white areas. (See **Did You Know?** on page 150 for more information about *Brown v. Board of Education*, the Supreme Court case that ended school segregation.)

Some African Americans, including Cobb, were allowed into mostly-white Chicago schools. She was in the honor society throughout high school. When it came time to choose a college, she decided to go to the University of Michigan to study biology.

The University of Michigan was segregated in 1941, when Cobb began her freshman year. African Americans lived together in one house. After three semesters, Cobb decided to transfer to Talladega (tal–ah–DAY–gah) College. It is a historically black college in Talladega, Alabama. The college did not accept transfer credits. Cobb took summer courses, studied hard, and graduated three–and–a–half years later, in 1944.

On the advice of a professor, Cobb applied to New York University, in New York City, to study biology. She applied for a teaching fellowship and was rejected. When she appeared at the university and asked again, though, her credentials[2] and her confidence impressed the professors. She began a teaching position that lasted for five years. In 1950, armed with a doctorate in cell biology, Cobb was ready to take on the world.

Her first job was at the Cancer Research Foundation of Harlem Hospital in New York City. Cell biology, Cobb's field, is the study of the cells of living things. She was interested in growing cancer cells in test tubes and studying how anticancer drugs affected them. To this day, Cobb says she is proudest of this research. It helped other scientists develop drugs to fight cancer.

Cobb was interested in a particular kind of cancer: melanoma, a type of skin cancer. Cobb wanted to find out whether melanin, the black or brown pigment[3] that colors skin, could

1. **boundaries** (BOWN-dreez) *n. pl.* lines that separate areas
2. **credentials** (crih-DEHN-shuhlz) *n. pl.* diplomas or other certificates that show evidence of ability
3. **pigment** (PIHG-muhnt) *n.* a coloring matter in plants and animals

shield the skin from the rays of the sun that are thought to cause melanoma. She thought that dark skins may have developed among people in sunny climates as protection from these rays.

In 1952, Cobb left New York to teach biology at the University of Illinois. She continued her research, though. Research "is never the same every day," she says. You choose the questions. You choose the challenges. Biological science, she says, is "the most exciting field in the world." But she loves teaching, as well. "You can see the electric light go on when kids understand what you're talking about," she says.

While in Illinois, she met and married Roy Cobb, an insurance salesman, in 1954. They have a son, Roy Jonathan, who was born in 1957. Cobb became known as a fine professor, as well as a talented researcher. From the University of Illinois, Cobb moved to Sarah Lawrence College, in Bronxville, New York, in 1960. She taught biology there for nine years. In 1967, Cobb and her husband divorced. She became a single mother.

In 1969, she became dean of Connecticut College. Somehow, she managed to keep up her research and teaching. She went to her lab every morning at 8, worked until 10, and then went to her dean's office. The research had to come first in the day, she says, because administration[4] was "an endless process. Paper, paper, paper." Finally, she was forced to give up research. "It required[5] a great deal of time."

While at Connecticut College, Cobb began a program to help minority students apply to medical and dental school. At least 90 percent of the 40 students in the program each year were accepted into medical or dental programs. Today, more than 20 colleges across the country use her program as a model.

In 1976, Cobb became dean of Douglass College, the women's college of Rutgers University in New Jersey. It was like being president of a college, she says, "because you [had] your own campus and faculty." Cobb also found time to address

---

4. **administration** (uhd-mihn-uh-STRAY-shuhn) *n.* the process of running an organization
5. **required** (rih-KWEYERD) *v.* took; needed

problems she saw nationwide. In 1979, she published an article called "Filters for Women in Science." In the article, she discussed the reasons that there are fewer women in science than men. To address this problem, she suggested supporting girls' interest in science beginning in elementary school. She also wanted to see more encouragement for girls to consider science careers.

Word of Cobb's abilities reached all the way to California. In 1981, she received a letter asking her to apply for the presidency of California State University at Fullerton, which had 24,000 students. She became the first African American woman to head a major public university on the West Coast.

That "first" role didn't bother Cobb, even though the university student body and faculty were mostly white. She "had a positive reception," she says. It was some time, however, before she felt the college community realized "that I had the experience and diplomacy"[6] to do a good job.

While at Cal State Fullerton, as the university is known, Cobb began two new schools: the School of Communication and the School of Engineering and Computer Science. She also persuaded[7] the California state legislature to pay for several new buildings, including a new science building, a new building for the study of old age, and the university's first dormitory.[8] Cobb felt that living on campus is an important part of learning. The residence hall bears her name.

Cobb resigned from Cal State Fullerton in 1990. She has 18 honorary doctorates, is on the board of many companies and foundations, and has won countless awards for her shining career. Her crusade now is helping more minority students to succeed. "I am angry at the condition of society that creates problems for blacks and women. But I think there are ways anger can be turned into something positive," she says. She has put her words

---

6. **diplomacy** (dih-PLOH-muh-cee) *n.* skill in dealing with people
7. **persuaded** (puhr-SWAYD-uhd) *v.* caused to do or believe something by argument; convinced
8. **dormitory** (DAWR-muh-tawr-ee) *n.* a building that houses students

into action, heading a center sponsored by the National Science Foundation that helps minority students into science and math careers. One program shows junior high school teachers new ways of teaching math and science. "When I see more black students in the laboratories than I see on the football field, then I'll be happy," Cobb says.

Her son, Roy, has taken his mother's interests to heart. When he was 14, Cobb gave him the field microscope her father had used when he was a medic in World World II. Today Roy is a doctor who practices in New Jersey. Like his mother, he has succeeded in a career that not many African Americans enter. Jewel Plummer Cobb is determined to change that. If her record is any indication, she may succeed.

> ***Did You Know?*** *In the fall of 1950, Linda Brown of Topeka, Kansas, was denied admission into an all-white neighborhood school. Linda's father, the Reverend Oliver Brown, turned to the NAACP and filed a suit against the Topeka school board. This case became known as* Brown v. Board of Education. *Arguing the case for Linda Brown before the Supreme Court was Thurgood Marshall, an NAACP lawyer who was himself appointed to the Supreme Court 16 years later. In 1954, the Supreme Court ruled in favor of the Browns. This ruling was the beginning of a civil rights revolution. It started the drive to integrate schools in the South, as well as public transportation, lunch counters, public buildings, and many other areas.* Brown v. Board of Education *is considered to be one of the most important Supreme Court decisions of the 20th century.*

AFTER YOU READ

EXPLORING YOUR RESPONSES

1. Cobb looked through a microscope and became fascinated with science. What experience have you had that may lead to a career?

2. Cobb studied cancer. What medical problem would you like to find a cure for? Why?

3. Which of Cobb's several careers interests you most? Why?

4. Cobb enjoyed teaching. Describe a teacher you enjoyed. What made him or her a good teacher?

5. Imagine that you had to design a program to get students interested in math and science. What would the program contain?

UNDERSTANDING WORDS IN CONTEXT

Read the following sentences from the biography. Think about what each underlined word means. In your notebook, write what the word means as it is used in the sentence.

1. She also learned, decades later, that Chicago kept most African Americans out of its schools by drawing boundaries around traditionally white areas.

2. She applied for a teaching fellowship and was rejected. When she appeared at the university and asked again, though, her credentials and her confidence impressed the professors.

3. The research had to come first in the day because administration was "an endless process," she says. "Paper, paper, paper."

4. Finally, she was forced to give up research. "It required a great deal of time."

5. She also <u>persuaded</u> the California state legislature to pay for several new buildings, including a new science building, a new building for the study of old age, and the university's first dormitory.

RECALLING DETAILS

1. How did Cobb become interested in science?

2. Describe Cobb's cancer research.

3. What programs has Cobb begun to help minority students?

4. What were Cobb's accomplishments at Cal State Fullerton?

5. What is Cobb doing now?

UNDERSTANDING INFERENCES

In your notebook, write two or three sentences from the biography that support each of the following inferences.

1. Cobb's family encouraged her to succeed.

2. Chicago's practice of segregating schools was unfair to African American children.

3. Cobb enjoys the challenges and discoveries of research.

4. Cobb doesn't mind doing things few African Americans have done before.

5. Cobb believes that minority students can succeed if they have encouragement.

INTERPRETING WHAT YOU HAVE READ

1. Why do you think Cobb decided to transfer to Talladega College?

2. Why do you think Cobb is proudest of the research she did at the Cancer Research Foundation?

3. Why do you think Cobb kept doing research and teaching while she was dean of Connecticut College?

4. Why do you think Cobb began the School of Communication and the School of Engineering and Computer Science at Cal State Fullerton?

5. Why do you think Cobb feels it is so important to involve more African Americans in math and science?

ANALYZING QUOTATIONS

Read the following quotation from the biography and answer the questions below.

"I am angry at the condition of society that creates problems for blacks and women. But I think there are ways anger can be turned into something positive," she says.

1. What "condition of society" is Cobb referring to?

2. What does this quote tell you about how Cobb deals with anger?

3. What are some ways that anger can be turned into something positive?

THINKING CRITICALLY

1. Why do you think Cobb thought she would go into dance or physical education?

2. How are the skills it takes to be a good researcher, administrator, and teacher similar? How are they different?

3. Why do you think Cobb was willing to be an administrator, a job she describes as "paper, paper, paper"?

4. How do you think Cobb convinced the community at Cal State Fullerton that she was a good president?

5. Why do you think Cobb would rather see African American students in the science laboratory than on the football field?

DONNA AUGUSTE

Donna Auguste writes on a Newton, the notebook-sized computer that she helped design for the Apple Computer Company. Auguste believes that computers can change the way people learn, shop, and communicate with others.

What features would you like to have in your computer? Perhaps you'd like to be able to carry it to class so that you could take notes. It would have to fit into your purse or backpack, and be lightweight. You wouldn't have room for a keyboard. It would be great, too, if the computer could read your handwriting. Imagine that. Well, Donna Auguste not only imagined such a computer—she designed and built it.

The Newton, as this new computer is called, signals just how much Auguste has helped revolutionize people's ideas about computers. But only three decades ago, she was a 4-year-old with one of her big sister's books. "I taught myself to read," says Auguste, who was born in Beaumont, Texas, in September 1958. Her mother, Willie Mae Fruge, who moved to Berkeley, California, when Auguste was 1 year old, did not have time to teach her about books. As a divorced parent with five daughters, she was busy working both as a telephone operator and as a waitress. She sometimes held two or three jobs at once.

Two of Auguste's sisters are older than she, and two are younger. "We'd get home from school and lock the door. My mother would call to make sure we'd made it home and then we'd sit at the kitchen table doing homework."

At 8 years of age, Auguste found a new hobby. "I'd take things apart; first doorknobs, then toasters. I wondered what made the heating element get hot and why the toast popped up." Curiosity led her to the doorbell, which she dismantled[1] with a butter knife. "In time I graduated to screwdrivers."

Her mother was not amused, Auguste recalls, but she was tolerant.[2] "In my family, people had great respect for differences. I wasn't teased or called a nerd."

---

1. **dismantled** (dihs-MAN-tuhld) *v.* took apart
2. **tolerant** (TAH-luh-ruhnt) *adj.* willing to respect or try to understand customs, ideas, or beliefs that are different from one's own

By the fifth grade, Auguste was building models of an *Apollo* spacecraft, which had been launched the year before, in 1968. She was identified by teachers as gifted. "I tested very high on state exams and some grown-ups would huddle around and discuss me. . . . I think they wouldn't have been so surprised if I'd been a boy."

Auguste believes that many people have difficulty accepting that girls can be as successful as boys at math, science, and engineering. "Some of the smartest kids in my science classes were girls," Auguste recalls, "but these girls didn't want to let on that they understood. It was considered a boys' kind of thing."

Life changed for Auguste in the seventh grade, when her class visited a science and technology museum. For the first time, she was able to touch a computer. Before that, she had only seen computers on television, during the Apollo mission. "Computers were a crucial[3] part of the voyage," says Auguste. No one she knew could tell her how computers worked. Unable to find library books on the subject, she returned to the museum as often as possible.

Two years after her initial trip to the museum, Auguste convinced her mother to let her enroll in the only public high school that offered a freshman computer class. It was located more than an hour away from the family home. "I was fascinated by the manner in which computers make life easier. Whatever you know how to do, computers can help you do better."

At 14, she took on a newspaper route. She began saving for college. No one in her family had attended college, and although they were encouraging, they were unable to offer her guidance. In her senior year, after earning high scores on her Scholastic Aptitude Test, Auguste received a letter from a college encouraging her to apply for a scholarship.

"We'd never heard of this place, and it was in Boston. I knew it would be cold, and the school had a name that sounded as if they taught baseball. Who'd ever heard of 'mit'? " She accepted a

---

3. **crucial** (KROO-shuhl) *adj.* extremely important

scholarship from the nearby University of California at Berkeley. Then she learned that "mit," or M.I.T., actually stood for the Massachusetts Institute of Technology, which has one of the premier[4] schools of engineering in the United States. Auguste says she is delighted with the way her life has turned out. She thinks, though, that it is important for students unfamiliar with how college works to join an organization that can answer questions about how to achieve in college. (See **Did You Know?** on page 159 for information on engineering and science support groups for minority students.)

In college, she ran into traditional biases[5] against women. "When professors told students to work in teams, I had a hard time finding partners. Most of the students were boys and they'd come right out and say they didn't want to work with a girl."

Auguste says that she never considered giving up. She graduated from Berkeley in 1980, with a degree in electrical engineering and computer science. She was the first member of her family to graduate from college. Continuing her studies in computer science, she attended Carnegie Mellon University in Pittsburgh, Pennsylvania, for three years, leaving before she attained an advanced degree.

Her first job out of graduate school was with a firm in northern California. She specialized in artificial intelligence, which involves developing similarities between the way humans think and computers work.

Auguste says she began to realize that whether a person is a man or a woman has little to do with how he or she is judged in the computer field. "They pay attention to what you can deliver. If you can get it out faster and better than anyone else, then you'll succeed."

One of her first professional challenges was with the 3M Corporation. The company had an expert scientist who knew more about how to mix adhesives than anyone else on the staff.

---

4. **premier** (prih-MIHR) *adj.* first in position or rank
5. **biases** (BEYE-uhs-ihz) *n. pl.* unreasonable judgments; prejudices

But he was about to retire. Management worried about finding someone to replace him. Auguste created a computer program that could suggest solutions for adhesive mixtures.

In 1991, Auguste was hired by the Apple Computer Company, which was also located in northern California. She led a team of 20 computer experts who spent months exploring new ideas for advanced computers. They wanted their creation to be lightweight and small. They also wanted to build a computer that could be used almost anywhere—even on a busy sidewalk.

After the team settled on what the computer should do, they went to work. It was a two-and-a-half-year effort, with Auguste's group growing to 60 experts. Auguste and others often worked 18 hours a day, seven days a week. As team manager, she made suggestions and decisions. She also guided other engineers and helped them work through technical problems.

The Newton was unveiled at Boston Symphony Hall in the summer of 1993. Computer experts and journalists from around the world came to see Apple's new hand-held computer. They learned that instead of pecking at keys with fingers, Newton users enter data into their computer with a special pen that has no ink. Handwriting is translated[6] into type on the screen. Combined with equipment such as a cellular phone, the Newton can follow commands like "Call Mom." Newton users can also be paged.

Auguste has since moved to a new company, U.S. West, in Boulder, Colorado. She is working on ways in which cable TV lines can be used to communicate with the world. For instance, a user might dial a shopping mall and select a sweater. The sweater would then be mailed to the user's home. Because information, not the shopper, travels back and forth to the store, this method of using computers is called the "information superhighway."

Away from the job, Auguste enjoys living in Colorado, where she can pursue her favorite hobby: horseback riding. She has purchased a new home that will, of course, have many computers, including a Newton.

---

6. **translated** (tranz-LAYT-uhd) *v.* changed; turned into

Auguste predicts that the homes of the future will be filled with computerized devices. "Even our light switches will understand individual differences. If I walk into a room, the computer will know I prefer table lamps. But if I come in with a business associate, it will also know that, in this case, I prefer overhead lights."

She believes computers will become a big part of homework. "They'll adjust to the rate of learning. I learned from my sisters that everyone learns at different rates. I may have learned to read earlier, but they learned other skills earlier than I did. The sister who became a nurse had no interest in medicine until she was 17. People learn at their own pace."

Thanks to Donna Auguste, children may be able to do just that. They may spend more time on a reading lesson that they find difficult, and move rapidly through an easier math lesson. They'll also get on-the-spot help, in the form of tutorials.[7] In this way, they might follow Auguste's example and reinvent the future.

> **Did You Know?** *Founded in 1974 with donations from major corporations, the National Action Council for Minorities In Engineering (NACME) has helped thousands of African American, Latino, and Native American students pursue careers in engineering. While the organization exists primarily to guide students toward careers in engineering, it can also help students who are interested in careers in science and math. NACME will send informative videos and even comic books, and can help locate engineering scholarships and corporate sponsorships. (See Career Resources on page 247 for more information on NACME.)*

---

7. **tutorials** (too-TAWR-ee-uhlz) *n. pl.* individual lessons

AFTER YOU READ

EXPLORING YOUR RESPONSES

1. Auguste's mother was not amused when she took objects apart to learn how they worked. What can someone learn by taking objects apart?

2. Auguste and her sisters locked the door and did their homework after school. How can working parents help their children manage their time after school?

3. Auguste believes many people have difficulty accepting the fact that girls can be successful in math, science, and engineering. Do you think girls can compete equally with boys in all fields? Explain.

4. August encountered bias in college. Tell of someone you know, or have read about, who dealt with bias.

5. Auguste says the future will be filled with computer devices. How would you like to see computers help you in school and everyday life?

UNDERSTANDING WORDS IN CONTEXT

Read the following sentences from the biography. Think about what each underlined word means. In your notebook, write what the word means as it is used in the sentence.

1. Curiosity led her to the doorbell, which she dismantled with a butter knife.

2. Her mother was not amused, Auguste recalls, but she was tolerant. "In my family people had great respect for differences."

3. Before that, she had only seen computers on television, during the Apollo mission. "Computers were a crucial part of the voyage," says Auguste.

4. Then she learned that "mit," or M.I.T., actually stood for the Massachusetts Institute of Technology, which has one of the premier schools of engineering in the United States.

5. In college she ran into traditional biases against women. ". . . Most of the students were boys and they'd come right out and say they didn't want to work with a girl."

RECALLING DETAILS

1. Why did Auguste teach herself to read?

2. As a child, why did Auguste take objects apart?

3. What biases did Auguste run into in college?

4. What are the key features of the Newton?

5. What is Auguste's latest project?

UNDERSTANDING INFERENCES

In your notebook, write two or three sentences from the biography that support each of the following inferences.

1. Auguste's mother taught her daughters about the value of hard work.

2. Auguste believes that computers can be useful in school.

3. Computers can change the way we live.

4. Auguste believes that bias is less often seen in the computer field.

5. The Newton is quite different from other computers.

INTERPRETING WHAT YOU HAVE READ

1. Why do you think Auguste became interested in computers?

2. Why do you think Auguste was fascinated by the science and technology museum?

3. How do you think Auguste's team decided on a design for the Newton?

4. How might using cable TV lines to shop help people and the environment?

5. Why do you think Auguste was so determined to succeed in the computer field?

ANALYZING QUOTATIONS

> *"[Computers will] adjust to the rate of learning. I learned from my sisters that everyone learns at different rates. I may have learned to read earlier, but they learned other skills earlier than I did. . . . People learn at their own pace."*

1. Describe a classroom in which students learn at their own pace.

2. What could a computer help you learn more easily?

3. If you could design a new computer, what features would it have?

THINKING CRITICALLY

1. Describe how some chore or form of entertainment has been changed by computers.

2. How did Auguste's mother serve as a role model?

3. What would be the advantages of communicating through cable TV? What would be the drawbacks?

4. Why do you think Auguste continued to take on new challenges even after achieving success with the Newton?

5. Do you think computers should be used in classrooms? Explain.

ROBERT MOSES

Robert Moses works with students at the Algebra Project, a program he designed. Moses links his work with students to his work in the Civil Rights Movement. He believes that people who know math have much greater hope for a successful future.

It was 1961. Three African American men walked slowly toward the courthouse in Amite County, Mississippi. Two were on their way to register to vote. Robert Moses was there to help. Three white men stood blocking the way. "Where are you going?" one asked. "To the registrar's[1] office," replied Moses. "No, you aren't," the man said, and jabbed Moses's forehead with the handle of his knife.

Moses staggered. The man hit him again, and again, bringing Moses to his knees. Blood flowed down his face. "We can't let something like this stop us," Moses said to his horrified companions. The three walked on, blood staining Moses's white shirt. When they got to the courthouse, the registrar gasped at the sight of Moses. Hurriedly, he closed the office. Once again, the officials who wanted to keep African Americans from voting had won. Eventually,[2] though, Moses and those fighting to gain voting rights for African Americans would succeed.

Robert Moses has never talked much about that day. He has never talked much about any of his acts of courage during the fight for voting rights. Instead, he has let his actions speak for him. Today, he is as passionate as ever about creating opportunities for African Americans, but his target has changed. Today, Moses is devoted to the cause of transforming[3] education. He calls his nationwide effort, the Algebra Project, "our version of civil rights 1992. But this time, we're organizing around literacy—not just reading and writing, but mathematical literacy." Today, Moses believes, mathematics is the crusade that can help poor Americans, particularly those from city schools, become respected, productive citizens.

1. **registrar** (REHJ-uh-strahr) *n.* an official keeper of records
2. **eventually** (ih-VEHN-choo-wuhl-ee) *adv.* finally; in the end
3. **transforming** (trans-FAWRM-ihng) *v.* changing the shape of something

Moses knows that children from poor neighborhoods can succeed if they get an education. He did it himself. He was born in New York City, in 1935. His family lived in one of the first public housing complexes in New York City, the Harlem River Project. His father was a janitor, his mother was a homemaker. His father had long been bitter that he was not able to get a good education, and he decided that his children would have more opportunities. When Moses, like his older brothers, proved gifted in mathematics, his parents pushed their three sons to take the test for admission to Stuyvesant High School, a very selective[4] school for gifted students, in lower Manhattan. All three passed.

Moses began living a divided life. By day, he traveled to Manhattan and his mostly white high school. At the end of the day, he would come back to his neighborhood in Harlem. There, African Americans formed a close community. Mothers talked while their children played outside. The children played baseball in the summer, and basketball at the Harlem YMCA in the winter.

After graduating from Stuyvesant, Moses went to Hamilton College in upstate New York on a scholarship. He was one of three African Americans in the student body. After the warm feeling of community in Harlem, the white, middle-class world of Hamilton was a shock. Moses was not invited into a fraternity, which provided most of the social life at the college. Instead, he dove into his classes. He began studying philosophy, a subject that explores the meaning of life.

Moses also became interested in pacifist thought—the belief that war and violence are never ways to solve problems. He spent one summer during his college years living with pacifists in France. He spent another summer in Japan, studying pacifism there. His professors in college were impressed. When he graduated, he was accepted into the Ph.D. program at Harvard University in Cambridge, Massachusetts, to study philosophy.

Two years later, his mother suddenly died. In shock, Moses went home for the funeral. Before he could return to school, the

---

4. **selective** (suh-LEHK-tihv) *adj.* choosing few out of many

police called. They had picked up his father wandering on the street. Moses left Harvard to take care of him. To support himself and his father, he took a job as a math teacher in a high school in New York City.

In 1960, Moses was still teaching when a few devoted people began trying to stop discrimination against African Americans in the South. Moses worked in the New York office of the Committee to Defend Martin Luther King. That summer, he took a bus to Atlanta to work for King. (See *Did You Know?* on page 168 for more information about Dr. Martin Luther King, Jr.)

When Moses arrived in the South, he spent some time in Atlanta. Then he decided to take on a job no one else thought could be done. He went to Mississippi to begin a one-man effort to sign up voters. With his quiet, insistent approach, Moses began to have an effect. At the end of the summer, though, he returned to his teaching post. He had one year left on his teaching contract, and he had to take care of his father.

He returned to Mississippi the next summer. His reputation grew. He became known as the calm man who just kept going. Despite being arrested many times, despite threats and beatings, he kept going. When the driver of a car in which he was riding was shot, Moses grabbed the steering wheel with one hand, put his arm around the driver's head with the other, and brought the out-of-control car to a halt. "In Mississippi, Bob Moses was the equivalent[5] of Martin Luther King," says historian Taylor Branch.

The fight for racial equality took its toll. At the end of the worst year, 1964, 4 people were dead, 80 had been beaten, and 67 churches, homes, and businesses had been destroyed. It was a bitter time. It was a hard time for Moses personally, as well. His marriage to Dona Richard, another civil rights worker, dissolved.

In 1966, he was drafted. Moses still believed strongly in pacifism, and he refused to fight in the Vietnam War. Instead, he fled to Canada. He was married again, to Janet Jemmott, another civil rights activist. In 1968, they moved to Tanzania, Africa,

---

5. **equivalent** (ih-KWIHV-uh-luhnt) *adj.* equal

where he taught high school math. "It was a good time to duck," Moses says now. "The idea that you can fight everything is crazy."

Eight years after going to Tanzania, Moses, his wife, and their four children returned to the United States. He went back to Harvard to complete his studies. His wife went to medical school. Soon, though, Moses found himself unhappy with the math instruction his daughter Maisha was receiving in school. He began to teach her math at home. "Doing math with my dad was part of our responsibility," Maisha says, "like taking out the garbage or doing the laundry." By eighth grade, though, Maisha hated being tutored at home. She wanted to rejoin her schoolmates. When Maisha's teacher invited Moses to teach algebra in 1982, he left his studies at Harvard and went back to teaching.

In 1980, Moses won a MacArthur Foundation grant—the so-called "genius" grants given to people to provide them with financial freedom so that they can work on special projects. Moses took advantage of that freedom to develop the Algebra Project. "What we're suffering from is a culture that says [that] to do well in math, you need to inherit genes from a parent who did well in math," Moses says. He is convinced that is wrong. What makes that attitude damaging, Moses says, is that math is the key to the future. Without algebra, students cannot get on the track to college. And without college, better-paying jobs are almost impossible to find.

Moses decided that teachers needed new ways of teaching algebra. As it was being taught, the subject had nothing to do with real life. The drills and exercises bored students. Moses designed a new way to teach algebra, based on the way people actually learn. Using his method, a student will look at an algebraic problem in real life, puzzle out a solution with friends, write about it, and then put it in mathematical terms.

Although some were unsure at first about Moses's method, they agree now that it seems to work. At Maisha's school in Cambridge, Massachusetts, the program has been in place for over a decade. When it began, very few students took the advanced test for mathematics, and few of them passed. Today, that school has the second-largest number of passing scores in the city. Since its founding 10 years ago, the Algebra Project has stretched across the country, reaching 9,000 students and gaining respect from educators nationwide.

To Moses, there is a clear link between the work he is doing now and the work from those long-ago days in Mississippi. "They didn't have the citizenship requirements of their age," he says of the barriers that kept African Americans from voting 30 years ago. "And so they were serfs,[6] absolutely without power. What is happening now is that we are watching the new serfs emerge," people with no knowledge of higher math and no hope of high-paying jobs. Like he did 30 years ago, Robert Moses is still organizing people for change. Back then, in his quiet way, he succeeded in helping African Americans gain the right to vote. Today, he is providing their sons and daughters the right to succeed.

> **Did You Know?** Dr. Martin Luther King, Jr., is one of the most important civil rights leaders of the 20th century. Born in 1929, he became nationally known for his belief in nonviolent resistance to segregation, and for his willingness to go to jail for his beliefs. His first well-known action against segregation was a successful year-long boycott in 1955 against the segregated public buses in Montgomery, Alabama. He also organized the 1963 March on Washington for civil rights, and the 1965 voter registration drive in Selma, Alabama. In 1964, he was awarded the Nobel Peace Prize. In 1968, he was shot and killed in Memphis, Tennessee, by James Earl Ray.

6. **serfs** (SERFZ) *n. pl.* slaves; servants

AFTER YOU READ

EXPLORING YOUR RESPONSES

1. Moses gave up teaching to fight for equal rights for African Americans. Would you give up a comfortable job to help others? Explain.

2. Moses was arrested and jailed while helping African Americans register to vote, but that did not stop him. What might you have done in this situation?

3. Moses does not like to boast about his accomplishments. Tell about someone you admire who has accomplished a great deal.

4. What do you think causes someone to brag?

5. Moses feels that knowing higher mathematics is critical today. Do you agree? Explain.

UNDERSTANDING WORDS IN CONTEXT

Read the following sentences from the biography. Think about what each underlined word means. In your notebook, write what the word means as it is used in the sentence.

1. Once again, the officials who wanted to keep African Americans from voting had won. Eventually, though, Moses and those fighting to gain voting rights for African Americans would succeed.

2. Today, he is as passionate as ever about creating opportunities for African Americans, but his target has changed. Today, Moses is devoted to the cause of transforming education.

3. When Moses, like his older brothers, proved gifted in mathematics, his parents pushed their three sons to take the test for admission to Stuyvesant High School, a very selective school for gifted students, in lower Manhattan.

4. "In Mississippi, Bob Moses was the <u>equivalent</u> of Martin Luther King," says historian Taylor Branch.

5. "They didn't have the citizenship requirements of their age," he says of the barriers that kept African Americans from voting 30 years ago. "And so they were <u>serfs</u>, absolutely without power."

RECALLING DETAILS

1. Why did Moses go to Mississippi?

2. Describe the racial separation Moses experienced during his school years.

3. Why did Moses begin to teach his daughter math at home?

4. How is teaching algebra similar to registering voters?

5. What evidence is there that Moses's approach to teaching algebra works?

UNDERSTANDING INFERENCES

In your notebook, write two or three sentences from the biography that support each of the following inferences.

1. Moses was not afraid to tackle problems others were unwilling to take on.

2. Moses has practiced pacifism.

3. Math helped Moses succeed.

4. Moses hopes that the Algebra Project will help poor children become successful in life.

5. Helping others is important to Moses.

INTERPRETING WHAT YOU HAVE READ

1. Why did Moses continue walking to the Mississippi courthouse when he was being beaten?

2. How might Moses's modesty have helped him become an effective leader?

3. What can you tell about Moses's feelings for his family from the biography?

4. What three adjectives do you think best describe Moses?

5. Why does Moses feel that voting is important?

ANALYZING QUOTATIONS

Read the following quotation from the biography and answer the questions below.

> *"What we're suffering from is a culture that says to do well in math, you need to inherit genes from a parent who did well in math."*

1. What does the quote tell you about Moses's attitude about learning math?

2. Why does he think this reasoning can be harmful?

3. How might a person change an idea like this?

THINKING CRITICALLY

1. Why do you think Moses became a successful leader?

2. If you had a chance to spend time with Moses during any period of his life, which period would you choose? Why?

3. Why would some whites want to keep African Americans from voting?

4. Moses describes people who could not vote as "serfs," and people who are not educated as the "new serfs." Why would he use this word to describe people?

5. If you were awarded a MacArthur Fellowship, explain how you might bring about social change.

CULTURAL CONNECTIONS

Thinking About What People Do

1. With a partner, choose one of the people in this unit. Write a short skit in which you act out a scene from that person's career. Use dialogue that helps tell the story. Present your skit to the class.

2. Imagine that you are president of an organization that is giving an award to one of the people in this unit. Write the speech you will give as you present the award. Tell about the work the person has done, why your group is making the award, and why this person deserves it. Then present your speech to the class.

3. Create a poster encouraging young people to go into one of the fields described in this unit. Use information from the biographies to make your poster educational. Use photographs and drawings to make it appealing. Highlight the benefits and attractions of that field. Display your poster in the classroom.

Thinking About Culture

1. Imagine that you are one of the people in this unit. Write a letter to a group of children, teaching them about "your" culture. Include facts from the person's biography and information from the sections entitled *Did You Know?*

2. What did you discover in this unit about overcoming barriers and problems? Do you think a person's cultural background can help both to create and to solve such problems? Give examples from the biographies to support your opinions.

3. In what ways did the parents of two of these subjects influence their child's life? Give examples.

Building Research Skills

Work with a partner to complete the following activity.

Find out more about one of the careers or fields discussed in this unit: biology, aerospace, medicine, computer technology, or mathematics. You may wish to select a career that you are considering for your future.

Schedule an interview with someone in your school or community who works in that field. Make a list of questions about the work he or she does. You might begin with the following questions:

> **Hint:** The Bibliography at the back of this book lists articles and books to help you begin your research.

☆ What jobs are available in this field?

☆ What classes would a person take in high school or college to prepare for this field?

> **Hint:** To gather more information, you might talk about the field with a guidance counselor at your school.

☆ What does a person in this field do in a typical day?

☆ What is the salary range for jobs in this field?

☆ Where could I write for more information about this field?

> **Hint:** Before you record an interview, discuss with the subject why the tape will be helpful to you. Make sure that he or she is willing to have the conversation recorded.

Go to the library to learn more about your chosen career. As you conduct your research, you may find additional questions you wish to ask your interviewee.

Next, conduct the interview. If the interviewee consents, you may wish to tape-record the interview. Take notes, too, to help you stay on track and to protect against tape failure. Share the findings from your interview in the form of an oral presentation. You may wish to play part of the tape to illustrate your report.

Extending Your Studies

MATH **Your task:** *To create a pie graph that shows your class's career preferences.* A pie graph illustrates the parts that make up a whole.

In this book, you can explore many careers. Which field do you find most interesting? Which fields do your classmates prefer? Use a pie graph to show the preferences of your class.

First, one person should count the number of students present in the class. Then, everyone should write his or her favorite career field on a small piece of paper. Use the general categories of *literature, communications, fine arts, performing arts, science, mathematics, business,* and *public service.* Each student may name only one field. A committee should count the students who have named each field, and write the totals on a piece of paper or on the chalkboard.

Next, create a class pie graph to present your findings. The whole graph, or "pie," represents all the students (100 %) in your class. Each "slice" of the pie represents the percentage of students that chooses each career. For example, if in your class of 30 people, 5 students prefer science, 7 want to go into public service, 3 prefer performing arts, 3 others want communications, and the rest are interested in business, your graph would look like the one below. Notice that the numbers were translated into percentages, and the pie was divided accordingly.

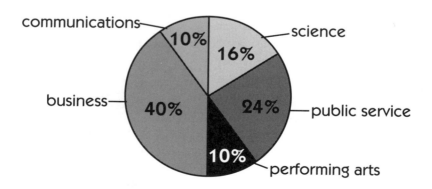

SOCIAL STUDIES **Your task:** *To make a brochure about an area.*
When Mae Jemison looked down on Earth from
her flight on the space shuttle *Endeavour,* she was
excited to see her hometown, Chicago.

Look at the map on page 1 of this book. Choose one location
that interests you. Make a list of the things you would like to learn
about that place. You might ask the following questions:

☆ What is the climate?

☆ Are there any historical landmarks in the area?

☆ Is the area urban, suburban, or rural?

☆ What kinds of industries or other jobs are available?

☆ What educational or cultural opportunities are available?

Go to the library to find answers to your questions. Use an
atlas, a tour book, and other reference materials to investigate the
area you have chosen. Chambers of commerce also may offer
brochures that describe the area.

Prepare a brochure, including five or six important or
interesting facts about the area. For each item, draw or copy a
picture and write a short description or explanation of the fact.
Use information that tells about the people, geography,
environment, climate, history, and culture of the area. Display
your brochure on your class bulletin board.

VISUAL ARTS **Your task:** *To design a logo for a company.* The
logo designed for Apple Computers, the
company that Donna Auguste worked for, is an
apple. The logo for NASA, for whom Mae
Jemison worked, is a space-age design of those letters.

Imagine that you own a high-tech company. Write a
paragraph that describes what your company does. Then design a
logo for the company. Remember that the best logos are simple
in design and use symbols rather than words.

WRITING WORKSHOP

In Unit 2, you wrote a biographical sketch about a friend or classmate. For this unit, you will write a **biographical sketch of someone in your family or community.** You might choose an aunt who is particularly special to you, or a doctor you know and admire. Your purpose in writing this biography is to show your friends and classmates why this person is special.

PREWRITING

In this **prewriting** step, you will gather information by conducting an interview. Here are suggestions for getting started:

Select a subject: First you must choose a subject. Think about the people in your family—not just those living with you, but other relatives as well. Someone in your community is also a possibility—perhaps someone who has done or achieved something special. In your notebook, jot down three or four names and some information about each person. Next, select the person who most interests you, who you think will interest others, and about whom you can gather information.

List questions: Think about what you already know about the person by listing some of your impressions. You might note the person's age, occupation, place of birth, or relationship to you. Jot down facts you can observe. Details like these will help you draw a clear picture of your subject. As you explore what you know, you will begin to see what you *do not* know. Start listing questions you have about the person. Focus on an important event in that person's life, and what he or she learned from it. Here are a few ideas for questions:

☆ What was the most important event in your life?

☆ Where did the event take place? Describe the place.

☆ What happened?

☆ What did you say and do?

☆ Who else was there?

☆ What did others say or do?

☆ How did you feel?

☆ What did you learn?

☆ Why was this event so special to you?

☆ Would you want to experience this event again? Explain.

Arrange for the interview: Set a time and a place that are convenient for both of you. Allow at least an hour.

Conduct the interview: Start with a question that cannot be answered with yes or no. You might begin, for example, with "Tell me about . . . ." Think about what your subject tells you. If he or she raises a question that you have not prepared, be ready to explore this new area. Take careful notes. If you want to record the interview, be sure to ask the subject's permission. Thank your subject when the interview is over.

Organize your notes: Decide on a main idea—the most important thing you learned from your subject. Underline details you will use. Then, in your notebook, write your subject's name, the event, and what he or she learned. For example:

> *Subject: Paul Benson, who is visually impaired.*
> *Event: Opened his own office as a psychologist.*
> *What he learned: Handicaps make goals challenging, but not impossible.*

DRAFTING

Once you have organized your notes and decided on a main idea, begin **drafting** your biography.

The Opening: You could begin with a quotation, either from the subject or from someone else. You could also begin by telling a story about the person. Whatever you choose, catch your reader's interest right away.

The Body: Here you will bring your subject to life through your description of the event. Remember that by showing what your subject says and does, and by describing how he or she looks, thinks, and feels, you let the reader "meet" your subject.

The Closing: By the end of your sketch, the reader should be able to "see" your subject and understand what he or she learned from the event. In our example, the subject learned that a handicap makes attaining goals challenging, not impossible.

> *A month after psychologist Paul Benson opened his practice, he was amazed at how many clients he had. "I'm a little surprised that they are willing to come to a visually impaired practitioner," he told a friend. "Why are you surprised?" the friend said. "Patients know that you don't need eyes to see people's feelings."*

REVISING

Put your biographical sketch aside for a day or two. Then, with the help of another student who will act as your editor, evaluate and **revise** your work. See the directions for writers and student editors below.

Directions for Writers: Before you give your sketch to a student editor, ask yourself the following questions:

☆ Does the opening hold the reader's interest?

☆ Do I give enough details to describe the event?

☆ Am I *showing,* not *telling,* the reader what happened?

☆ Does the dialogue sound natural?

☆ Does the ending sum up what my subject learned, and leave the reader with a lasting impression?

Make notes for your next draft or revise your work before you give it to your student editor. Then ask your student editor to read your work. Listen carefully to his or her suggestions. If they seem helpful, use them to improve your writing when you revise.

Directions for Student Editors: Read the work carefully and respectfully, remembering that your purpose is to help the writer do his or her best work. Keep in mind that an editor should always make positive, helpful comments that point to specific parts of the sketch. After you read the work, use the following questions to help direct your comments:

☆ What do I like most about the biographical sketch?

☆ Can I see the person or event in my mind?

☆ What would I like to know more about?

PROOFREADING

When you are satisfied that your work says what you want it to say, **proofread** it for errors in spelling, punctuation, capitalization, and grammar. Also look for phrases that can be improved. Use the chart below as a guide. Then make a neat, final copy of your autobiographical essay.

Needs Improvement	Revised
Ben is the best player we have.	Ben is the best quarterback our team has ever had.
Maria felt sad.	Maria felt as if she had lost her best friend.
The audience liked the show.	The audience clapped wildly and gave the band a standing ovation.

PUBLISHING

After you revise your sketch, you are ready to **publish** it. Illustrate your finished copy with drawings, a collage, or photographs. Make your biographical sketch available for other students to read in a library of Very Important People.

AFRICAN AMERICANS IN BUSINESS AND PUBLIC SERVICE

In this unit, you will read about five African Americans who kept their goals in sight no matter what obstacles were put in their way. Read to discover what personal strengths, talents, and interests they have in common, as well as what sets them apart.

Basketball great **Julius Erving** talks about the importance of a positive outlook. "A lot of people that I grew up with had the same opportunities that I had. . . ." he says. "They didn't realize that your goals will determine what you're going to be."

College president **Johnnetta Cole**'s mother counseled her to choose a career that would satisfy her. She said, "If you do work that you hate, you will be miserable for the rest of your life. Find work that you love."

NAACP leader **Benjamin Chavis** agrees that attitude is important. He says, "One of the things I learned from Dr. Martin Luther King, Jr., is that there is no room for bitterness. You can't take that baggage around with you."

Ebony publisher **John Johnson** thinks that people can succeed, no matter what their circumstances are. He says, "Men and women are limited not by the place of their birth, not by the color of their skin, but by the size of their hope."

Children's rights advocate **Marian Wright Edelman** advises that a person's heritage can inspire him or her to succeed. She has written, "Remember your roots, your history, and the forebears' shoulders on which you stand."

As you read these biographies, consider how self-confidence, a positive outlook, and pride in one's heritage have helped each person to succeed.

JULIUS ERVING

Basketball Hall of Famer Julius Erving plays for the Philadelphia 76ers. Erving pioneered the art of leaping and dunking in basketball. He is still a pioneer today, using his skills in business and in many charities.

The orange ball landed in his hands as if it had come home. Without a pause, the man jumped, seeming to stay in the air, to just hang there. Beneath him, the other players watched. The man twisted in the air, and shot the ball. It dropped into the net without a sound. The crowd was on its feet. Once more, cheers rang in the auditorium. Dr. J., Julius Erving, had done it again. "Doc goes up and never comes down," said his wondering teammate, New York Nets player Bill Melchionni.

Julius Erving changed the game of basketball. Today's stars can leap and dunk, but the man who pioneered the art form was Erving. Today, when basketball fans trade names of the players who made a difference, Julius Erving is always on the list. Perhaps as important, he is on other lists as well. He is a successful businessman, a devoted father, a legendary team leader. He is also a man who has always used his skills, talents, and time to help others. Julius Erving is truly a star. (See *Did You Know?* on page 187 for more information on African Americans in professional basketball.)

Erving, however, did not begin his life in luxury. He was born in Hempstead, Long Island, in 1950. He had an older sister, Alexis, and a younger brother, Marvin. When Erving was 3, his father left the family. Erving's mother, Callie Mae Erving, was one of 14 children of South Carolina sharecroppers. To support the family, she found work as a domestic.

For most of his childhood, the Ervings lived in a low-income housing project. Callie Mae Erving ruled the family with love and "the desire to make each day better than the one before and to improve each task, however small," she later told an interviewer.

Julius Erving agrees. "My family survived because we had determination and a positive outlook," Erving says. "A lot of people I grew up with had the same opportunities that I had but they didn't have the same attitude. They just thought they'd do nothing, like everybody else—they would hang around and that would be it. They didn't realize that your goals will determine what you're going to be. I saw that basketball could be my way out and I worked hard to make sure it was."

Erving didn't rely only on basketball to make his way, though. Although Erving thought of himself as a loner, he pushed himself to get involved. "I always believed in myself. Even when I was a kid, before I started playing basketball, I felt I could hold my own in communicating with other people." While in elementary school, Erving began reciting poetry—and winning awards at poetry reading contests.

Soon, however, Erving's gift for basketball became clear. "Whether basketball chose me, or I chose it, I still don't know," he says. "I think it's the former—it chose me." A director at the park where Erving played told the coach of the local Salvation Army team about his talent. Today there is a plaque[1] marking the Roosevelt playground where Erving practiced. Erving began to play for the Salvation Army team when he was 10, scoring 11 points on average in each game. Two years later, the team won the county basketball association championship.

When Erving was 13, his mother remarried. She and her children moved into her new husband's home in a town not far from Hempstead. As a high school student, Erving quickly became a star. What his coach, Ray Wilson, remembers was a player with unusual ability and unusual maturity.[2] "He came to us almost as he is today," Wilson said in 1983. "And he is [even] a much better person than he is a basketball player."

He was a fine basketball player. He played on all-star teams, and in several state tournaments. But his maturity was tested when his younger brother, Marvin, died of the blood disease lupus when he was 16. "When he died I stopped fearing and I stopped crying," Erving said in 1975. "Right now, I don't think there is anything that can make me cry."

As he approached graduation, with a B average and an outstanding talent for playing basketball, Erving was wooed by

1. **plaque** (PLAK) *n.* a thin piece of metal that honors a person
2. **maturity** (muh-TOOR-uht-ee) *n.* being older and having wisdom

several colleges. Erving chose the University of Massachusetts. During his first year, he broke the freshman record for scoring and rebounding. His record-breaking performance continued for two more years. Before his senior year in college, Erving dropped out to become a professional player. He later went back to college, though, and graduated, putting into practice what he tells hopeful basketball stars: Education is important. "There's nothing wrong with dreaming, shooting in that direction, but don't put all your eggs in one basket."

When he decided to turn pro, Erving was pursued by professional scouts. Although he was 6'6", several inches shorter than most of those guarding him, his size did not seem to matter. He signed a lucrative[3] contract with the American Basketball Association's Virginia Squires. In 1971-72, his first professional year, he was sixth in the league in scoring. The next season, he led the league.

Next, he went to the New York Nets, where he played until the 1976-77 season. When he joined them, the Nets were an obscure[4] team. That soon changed. It was in New York that Erving's reputation began to soar as high as his jump shot. "He handles a basketball the way an average person handles a tennis ball," said *The New York Times.* "He can raise one arm above other players' two outstretched hands and snatch the ball away as if he were taking a handful of popcorn." Given a running start, he could leap 15 feet, fake passes several times while in mid-air, and put the ball through the hoop while the much taller guard was still off-balance. Watching Erving was more like watching an athletic ballet than a basketball game. Temple University even gave him an honorary doctorate in dance.

It was during these days that Erving gained the nickname Dr. J. The doctor was a holdover from high school. Erving had called a friend on the basketball team "professor." The friend called Erving "doctor" in return. When he got to the Nets, his

---

3. **lucrative** (LOO-kruh-tihv) *adj.* producing wealth
4. **obscure** (ahb-SKYOOR) *adj.* relatively unknown

teammates shortened the name to Dr. J. Later, basketball fans joked that when this doctor operated, "he buried his patients."

Erving was more than a superb player. He was the glue that held the team together. Erving seemed to feel he had a mission to help the younger players cope with the fast-paced life they led. "I was very conscious of the stereotypes associated with black athletes," Erving says. "It was embarrassing to see a guy struggling through an interview. I always felt if I made it, I wanted to help eradicate[5] that and maybe protect some of them."

Rod Thorn, who worked as an assistant coach with the Nets, says, "Of all the great players, Julius understood the team thing best. We had a lot of young, unstable guys on that Nets team, but as long as Julius was there, they stayed in line. He looked out for them. They respected him."

In 1976, Erving was traded to the Philadelphia 76ers, where he played for 11 years and continued his remarkable exploits[6] on the court. He drew enormous crowds, and averaged 22 points a game. During his career, he scored 30,000 points. He was only the third player in ABA-NBA history to do so. In 1987, Erving retired. In 1993, the first year he was eligible, he was inducted[7] into the Basketball Hall of Fame. "I am thankful to the millions of fans who, with my family and friends, touched me emotionally and spiritually," he said at the ceremony. "I carry a feeling of oneness with them into these hallowed[8] halls."

Since his retirement from basketball, Erving has been doing one thing he could not do while he was playing. He spends time with his family. As close as his basketball family was to him, Erving cherishes his real family. In 1972, he married Turquoise Brown. Today, they have four children. "My greatest hobby," he says, "is just watching my kids grow."

---

5. **eradicate** (ih-RA-duh-kayt) *v.* eliminate; do away with
6. **exploits** (EHK-sploits) *n. pl.* deeds; acts
7. **inducted** (ihn-DUKT-uhd) *v.* admitted as a member
8. **hallowed** (HAL-ohd) *adj.* sacred; greatly respected

Besides that, Erving has become a successful businessman. He owns a Coca-Cola franchise[9] in Philadelphia, and runs his own management company. He has told the NBA he would like to be considered if an NBA team is up for sale. And, as he always has, Erving gives time and money to charities. He raises money for the Lupus Foundation, remembering the brother he lost so many years ago. He also created a college scholarship fund in Marvin's name for city youth. He has set up recreation programs for inner city children, and given money to New York University Medical Center, the United Negro College Fund, and the Salvation Army. He has won an armful of awards for his contributions, from organizations such as the Urban League, *Ebony* magazine, Easter Seals, and the Lupus Foundation.

In 1988, a year after his retirement from professional basketball, a bronze statue of Julius Erving was unveiled outside The Spectrum, the stadium where he played for Philadelphia. "When you look at this statue, see more than just a former athlete," Erving told the crowd when the statue was unveiled. "See someone who considers himself your brother, your friend." The larger-than-life statue gleams in the sun. On it is inscribed, "Athlete-Sportsman-Gentleman."

> ***Did You Know?*** *Although the first professional basketball league was established in the United States in the mid-1930s, African Americans were not drafted into the leagues for another 15 years. Chuck Cooper, a forward, signed a contract with the Boston Celtics in 1951. By 1964, most National Basketball Association teams had at least five African American players. By 1974, African American players were dominating the game. That trend has continued.*

---

9. **franchise** (FRAN-cheyez) *n.* a license to sell products in a certain area

AFTER YOU READ

EXPLORING YOUR RESPONSES

1. Tell about a sports figure or other well-known person whose work you admire.

2. Although Erving grew up in poverty, he kept a positive outlook on life. How can a positive attitude help people achieve their goals?

3. When Erving's mother remarried, he moved to a different neighborhood and a new school. How might changes like these affect a teenager's life?

4. Some of Erving's teammates had difficulty adjusting to their new "fast-paced life." What difficulties do you think he means?

5. Do you think professional athletes should donate time and money to help those who are less fortunate? Explain.

UNDERSTANDING WORDS IN CONTEXT

Read the following sentences from the biography. Think about what each underlined word means. In your notebook, write what the word means as it is used in the sentence.

1. What his coach, Ray Wilson, remembers was a player with unusual ability and unusual maturity. "He came to us almost as he is today," Wilson said in 1983.

2. Although he was 6'6", several inches shorter than most of those guarding him, his size did not seem to matter. He signed a lucrative contract with the American Basketball Association's Virginia Squires.

3. "It was embarrassing to see a guy struggling through an interview. I always felt that if I made it, I wanted to help eradicate that and maybe protect some of them."

4. In 1976, Erving was traded to the Philadelphia 76ers, where he played for 11 years and continued his remarkable exploits on the court. He drew enormous crowds, and averaged 22 points a game.

5. In 1993, the first year he was eligible, he was inducted into the Basketball Hall of Fame.

RECALLING DETAILS

1. How was Erving able to become successful despite growing up in a family where there was little money?

2. Why was Erving so heavily recruited by various colleges?

3. Name two ways that Erving used his success to help others.

4. How did Erving change the game of basketball?

5. In what charitable activities is Erving active?

UNDERSTANDING INFERENCES

In your notebook, write two or three sentences from the biography that support each of the following inferences.

1. Even as a young boy, Erving had confidence in his abilities.

2. Erving's determination and positive attitude were important to his success.

3. The death of Erving's brother affected him deeply.

4. Making it to the professional ranks requires hard work.

5. Being a team player means caring for others.

INTERPRETING WHAT YOU HAVE READ

1. How do you think Erving's mother affected his life?

2. How do you think Erving's life was affected by growing up in a housing project?

3. How did Erving help the younger players on his team?

4. Why does Erving urge youngsters who dream of becoming basketball stars to "not put all their eggs in one basket"?

5. Why does Erving think education is important even for professional athletes?

ANALYZING QUOTATIONS

Read the following quotation from the biography and answer the questions below.

> "A lot of people that I grew up with had the same opportunities that I had but they didn't have the same attitude. They just thought they'd do nothing, like everybody else—they would hang around and that would be it. They didn't realize that your goals will determine what you're going to be."

1. How was Erving's attitude different from that of some of the people around him?

2. Why do you think some people from similar backgrounds succeed, while others do not?

3. Do you agree that "your goals determine what you're going to be"? Explain.

THINKING CRITICALLY

1. Erving led his teams to winning records. How do you think one person can help a team succeed?

2. What Erving lacked in height, he made up for in athletic skills. How can a person overcome obstacles to success?

3. In high school, Erving maintained a B average. Why might good grades be important to an athlete?

4. How might education and effective communication help a person in business?

5. What kind of charitable work might you set up to help others? Explain.

JOHNNETTA COLE

Johnnetta Cole, president of Spelman College in Atlanta, Georgia, inspects African figures at a gift shop. Cole uses her knowledge of anthropology in her role as a college president to help her create a community that is respectful of others' ideas and cultures.

It was the first day of class. The professor began moving his body to Jamaican music. As he swayed, he talked about the rhythm of the music. He talked about how those rhythms became part of African American culture. His words hit Johnnetta Cole like a thunderbolt. By the time the professor stopped talking, Cole's life had changed.

Ever since she was a child, Cole had thought she wanted to be a doctor. But that day in 1953, as she listened to this professor at Oberlin College describe cultural anthropology—the study of how people live, including the way they eat, work, worship, and play—she knew she had discovered what she wanted to do with her life. For the first time, she says, she saw how to create "the tools to better understand and gain some perspective on my experience." All her life, she had questioned what it meant to be African American in the United States. Through anthropology, she thought, she might find answers to those questions.

Cole became an anthropologist whose influence has ranged far beyond the classroom. In 1987, she became the first African American woman to serve as president of Spelman College, a historically black college for women that was founded in 1881. (See **Did You Know?** on page 195 for more information about historically black colleges.)

Cole was born Johnnetta Betsch in 1936, in Jacksonville, Florida, to the most prominent[1] African American family in town. A.L. Lewis, one of the founders of the first insurance company in Florida, was her great-grandfather. He began the company to help African American families pay for funeral expenses. Before A.L. Lewis founded the Afro-American Industrial and Benefit Association in 1901, people whose relatives had died asked friends to help pay for the funeral. "Folks

---

1. **prominent** (PRAHM-uh-nehnt) *adj.* well-known; important

in Jacksonville, Florida, still talk about how A.L. Lewis, the son of slaves, entered the work world as a water boy for a Jacksonville sawmill and built something for his family and his people," Cole says.

Studying anthropology helped Cole understand that her great-grandfather's business was founded in the tradition of the Sou, an African culture. In this tradition, each community member makes a regular contribution to a fund. When one member needs money, he or she receives the whole amount. The fund is then begun again.

By the time Cole was born, to John Thomas Betsch, Sr., and Mary Frances Lewis Betsch, A.L. Lewis was a legend in Jacksonville. His name graced the A.L. Lewis Library and the A.L. Lewis YWCA. Knowing her great-grandfather, Cole has written, "could not help but shape my consciousness." His spirit, she says, "taught me that we African Americans can and must do for ourselves." Cole grew up reading literature and listening to classical music. Although her mother had been an English professor and her father an independent businessman, both soon were working for the family business. Her mother became Vice-President and Treasurer of the Afro-American Life Insurance Company.

The family's wealth helped them escape some of the pain of racism, Cole says. "As children we were driven everywhere to spare us from the humiliation of the back of the bus." When her family wanted to buy clothes, they would arrange for fittings. Other African Americans would be refused the right to do so. But, Cole says, "I knew at an early age that there was, as is the case today, no amount of money or status that could shelter African Americans from racism. . . ."

Cole also remembers having to leave her family when she was 8. The local school board had decided that African American children did not need to be educated for a full day. Cole and her sister Marvyne were sent to Washington, D.C., so that they could get a full day of school. "I wanted to be at home with my Mom and Dad, and I knew what prevented this was racism," she says.

When she was 15, she tested for early college admission and entered Fisk University in Nashville, Tennessee. Fisk opened up the world of African American thinkers and artists for Cole. In 1953, though, Cole's father died. "I was devastated by the loss," she says. "Hurt, confused, lonely, I decided to leave Fisk and transfer to Oberlin College," which her sister was attending.

Oberlin, Cole says, was "a culture shock." The college was alive with many different types of people, but few were African American. "I was part of a little band of Black folk in a White sea," Cole writes.

Then Cole discovered anthropology. "How in the world are you ever going to make a living doing something like that?" her grandfather asked. Cole burst into tears. Her mother tried to comfort her. Then, she says, her mother looked at her and said, "But if you do work that you hate, you will be miserable for the rest of your life. Find work that you love. If this is your passion, follow it."

Cole did. She remembers "gasping with shock and joy" after reading that perhaps Africans hadn't given up the customs[2] of their ancestors[3] when they were enslaved in the United States. Instead, they had brought those customs along and made them part of life in this country. "Forty years ago," she says, "such thinking was revolutionary." Cole felt liberated[4] by the connections she found between African and African American cultures. There were, for example, the similarities between the cultures in "our body movement—the way we gesture, walk, and dance." To her, the connections showed "how terribly human we all are. Just as Europeans had brought their cultures and ways of life to America, so, too, had Africans."

Cole earned her master's and doctoral degrees from Northwestern University in Evanston, Illinois. While there, she met and, in 1960, married another graduate student, Robert Cole. They had three sons. They divorced in 1982. Some years later, Cole married Art Robinson, a childhood friend.

---

2. **customs** (KUHS-tuhmz) *n. pl.* ways of behaving that are passed down from one generation to the next
3. **ancestors** (AN-sehs-tuhrz) *n. pl.* people from whom one is descended
4. **liberated** (LIHB-uh-ray-tuhd) *v.* set free

During her career as an anthropologist, Cole worked as a professor at Washington State University, the University of Massachusetts at Amherst, and Hunter College in New York. Because of her achievements as a professor, she was asked to apply for college presidencies. It was not until the presidency of Spelman became available, though, that she applied. Here, she thought with excitement, she could not only show African American women what they could achieve—she could help make it happen. Cole has done that, and more. She established an International Affairs Center at Spelman, as well as several other innovative[5] programs. One matches Spelman students with mentors from Atlanta's business community. There are also faculty exchanges between Spelman and such major institutions as Princeton and New York University. In 1992, Spelman was named the number one regional liberal arts college in the South by *U. S. News & World Report.*

Cole says that Spelman is a place that is "fundamentally[6] free of racism and sexism." That is her vision for the world. "And though it is sometimes very difficult to imagine our nation totally free of racism and sexism, my intellect, my heart, and my experience tell me that is it actually possible," she says. "For that day when neither exists, we must all struggle."

> ***Did You Know?*** *More than 100 years ago, colleges began to open to provide higher education for African Americans. The first of these colleges, Cheyney State in Pennsylvania, was founded in 1837. Today, these institutions number more than 100 and can be found in 19 states, mostly in the South. In 1964, over half of all African American college students attended historically black colleges and universities. Currently, more than 200,000 African American students attend historically black colleges and universities.*

---

5. **innovative** (IHN-uh-vay-tihv) *adj.* something new or changed
6. **fundamentally** (fun-duh-MEHNT-tuh-lee) *adv.* basically; essentially

AFTER YOU READ

EXPLORING YOUR RESPONSES

1. Cole's study of anthropology taught her about her African roots. How can learning about one's roots make a difference in the way someone feels about himself or herself?

2. What might the advantages be to belonging to one of the most prominent families in town? What might the disadvantages be?

3. Cole first considered studying medicine, but changed to anthropology. How should a person decide on a career?

4. Cole has written that no amount of money or status can shelter African Americans from racism. Do you agree? Explain.

5. How do you think it might feel to be one of only a few members of a cultural group in a school or community?

UNDERSTANDING WORDS IN CONTEXT

Read the following sentences from the biography. Think about what each underlined word means. In your notebook, write what the word means as it is used in the sentence.

1. Cole was born Johnnetta Betsch in 1936, in Jacksonville, Florida, to the most prominent African American family in town.

2. She remembers "gasping with shock and joy" after reading that perhaps Africans hadn't given up the customs of their ancestors when they were enslaved in the United States.

3. Cole felt liberated by the connections she found between African and African American culture. There were, for

example, the similarities between the cultures in "our body movement—the way we gesture, walk, and dance."

4. She established an International Affairs Center at Spelman, as well as several other <u>innovative</u> programs.

5. Cole says that she is happy at Spelman because it is a place that is "<u>fundamentally</u> free of racism and sexism." That is her vision for the world.

RECALLING DETAILS

1. What is cultural anthropology?

2. Why did Cole's great-grandfather form an insurance business?

3. What attitude did Cole's family have about education?

4. What connections did Cole find between African and African American cultures?

5. Why did Cole decide to become president of Spelman?

UNDERSTANDING INFERENCES

In your notebook write two or three sentences from the biography that support each of the following inferences.

1. Cole's great-grandfather believed that African Americans must help themselves.

2. Cole sees anthropology as a way for people to understand themselves.

3. Cole's mother believes that there are things more important than money in choosing a career.

4. Like her great-grandfather, Cole believes she should help her community.

5. Cole believes there are basic similarities between peoples.

INTERPRETING WHAT YOU HAVE READ

1. How did Cole's family's wealth affect her life?

2. How can anthropologists help unite the people of the world?

3. How might reading about African customs have made Cole think differently about African American culture?

4. Cole says that neither success nor wealth can shelter African Americans from racism. Explain what she meant.

5. Why do you think Cole felt liberated by the connections between Africa and African American cultures?

ANALYZING QUOTATIONS

Read the following quotation from the biography and answer the questions below.

> *"Just as Europeans had brought their cultures and ways of life to America, so, too, had Africans."*

1. Name some traditions that Europeans brought to America.

2. Why might it have mattered to Cole that her own culture and traditions had been brought from Africa?

3. What are the pros and cons of having a strong cultural identity?

THINKING CRITICALLY

1. Why do you think A.L. Lewis felt it was so important for African Americans to "do for ourselves"?

2. What characteristics would help a person succeed as an anthropologist?

3. How might a background in anthropology help a college president?

4. Cole established a program at Spelman that matches students with mentors from the business community. How might such a program help a student?

5. Cole believes that a world without racism is possible. Do you agree? Explain.

BENJAMIN CHAVIS

Benjamin Chavis, the executive director of the National Association for the Advancement of Colored People (NAACP), announces the opening of the first Latino chapter of that organization in May, 1993. Chavis welcomes members of all culture groups who want to work for social justice.

At a family ceremony after Sunday dinner, when Benjamin Chavis (CHAY-vihs) was 12 years old, his father presented him with a membership card to the National Association for the Advancement of Colored People (NAACP). Chavis, who was born in Oxford, North Carolina, in 1948, remembers feeling that being given that card was "part of my initiation[1] into manhood." (See **Did You Know?** on page 203 for more information about the NAACP.)

Chavis experienced another kind of initiation also. He went into the public library and asked to borrow a book. Chavis knew that library was open only to white people. But the books available in the library for the town's African Americans were usually worn hand-me-downs, often with missing pages.

The librarian told Chavis to leave. Then she called his parents. He was determined, however, to borrow a library book that had both covers. His one-child protest caused great attention. Eventually, the library was opened to all of Oxford's citizens. For Chavis, one of five children born to Benjamin Chavis, Sr., a brick mason, and Elisabeth Chavis, a schoolteacher, it was the first of many such courageous stands.

Chavis's actions grew out of a proud family heritage[2] of commitment to education and justice. John Chavis, Benjamin's great-great-grandfather, was a freed man who had been educated at Princeton University in Princeton, New Jersey. During the day, John Chavis taught at an academy for the children of slaveholders. But at night he taught enslaved parents and children. In 1845, it was illegal for anyone to educate enslaved people. John Chavis was caught, and fatally beaten by a mob.

---

1. **initiation** (ih-nihsh-ee-AY-shuhn) *n.* admittance to a club or group with a special ceremony

2. **heritage** (HEHR-uht-ihj) *n.* something that is handed down from one's ancestors

The academy where he taught later became the University of North Carolina. John Chavis's grandson, Ben, would graduate from that school with a bachelor's degree in chemistry in 1970, 124 years later.

During the 1960s, thousands of African Americans throughout the South demanded their rights to full citizenship. While Chavis was still in college, the Civil Rights Movement offered him many opportunities to prove that he had the ability to become a strong leader.

A meeting with Dr. Martin Luther King, Jr., encouraged him to become a student activist.[3] Chavis rallied students to work with civil rights organizations on behalf of municipal[4] workers in several Southern cities. Many of these employees were sanitation workers who earned lower wages and had poorer working conditions than white municipal workers. "My leadership style is to organize . . . people at the grass-roots level," he says. Often, this meant finding out what the workers' needs were and taking their complaints to the city council and the mayor.

Chavis remained committed to fighting for the rights of others after graduating in 1970. That year, he became an ordained minister of the United Church of Christ. He also took a position teaching high school chemistry in Wilmington, North Carolina, in 1970. Then a series of tragic incidents took away his freedom for several years. They also nearly destroyed his life.

While organizing a church-sponsored boycott[5] of segregated schools, an African American protester was shot to death by police. A short while later, a white-owned grocery store was firebombed. Chavis and several protesters were suspects.

The Wilmington police chief ordered Chavis to leave town. When he refused, Chavis and nine other people were arrested and convicted for arson, assault, and conspiracy to murder. The trial was known nationwide as the Wilmington Ten Case.

---

3. **activist** (AK-tih-vuhst) *n.* one who takes direct action to achieve a goal
4. **municipal** (myoo-NIHS-uh-puhl) *adj.* relating to local government
5. **boycott** (BOI-kaht) *n.* a refusal to buy, sell, or use a product or service in order to express disapproval

In 1972, while he was out on bail and awaiting trial, his car was firebombed. Chavis was hospitalized with severe burns. During his imprisonment, he was occasionally placed in leg irons, despite the discovery of a plot among some prison guards to murder him. After Chavis had served four-and-a-half years, three witnesses admitted that they had lied at the trial. An appeals court ordered Chavis and the others to be released.

Despite having endured many hardships while in prison, Chavis refused to be bitter.[6] "One of the things I learned from Dr. Martin Luther King, Jr., is that there is no room for bitterness," he says. "You can't take that baggage around with you."

Chavis used his time in prison well. He wrote a book, *An American Political Prisoner Appeals for Human Rights*, and earned a Master of Divinity degree from Duke University. In the years since his release, he has earned a Ph.D. in theology from Howard University, in Washington, D.C., and a Ph.D. in philosophy from Union Theological Seminary in New York City.

Chavis also emerged from this experience with an even deeper commitment to the causes in which he believes. For 25 years, he worked for the United Church of Christ Commission for Racial Justice, a civil rights organization that is based in Cleveland, Ohio. He became its executive director in 1985.

In this position, Chavis headed the first national environmental summit[7] for people of color. The event brought together more than 800 leaders from the African American, Latino, Asian, and Native American communities. The purpose of the summit was to set an agenda[8] for environmental justice. The summit found that many of the greatest industrial polluters and toxic-waste dump sites in the United States are located in communities where people of color live.

When the NAACP began a nationwide search for an executive director and chief executive officer, they looked to

6. **bitter** (BIHT-uhr) *adj.* intensely unpleasant
7. **summit** (SUM-iht) *n.* a conference of high officials
8. **agenda** (uh-JEN-duh) *n.* a list or plan of things to be considered or done

Ben Chavis. According to William Gibson, chairman of the board of the NAACP, "This man is a proven civil rights champion. He has truly lived the life of the struggle."

In April 1993, Chavis, who is married and the father of six children, became the seventh person, and the youngest, to head the nation's oldest and largest civil rights organization. Four days after his appointment, he flew from Baltimore, Maryland, where the NAACP has its headquarters, to Los Angeles. His purpose was to meet with former gang members and youth leaders. A week later, he attended a "peace summit" with 200 gang members in Kansas City, Missouri. "I'm not a stranger to the 'hood," he says. "These young brothers and sisters need attention."

Since taking on the job at the NAACP, Chavis has begun to define the civil rights issues that are important to African Americans in the 1990s. Near the top of the list, he believes, is the urgent need to attract more young people to become members. Under his leadership, this has already begun to take place. According to Chavis, 64% of the NAACP's new members are under the age of 24. Membership in the NAACP, Chavis states, is not limited to African Americans. He welcomes everyone who wants to work for justice.

> ***Did You Know?*** *The National Association for the Advancement of Colored People (NAACP) was formed in 1911. That was 49 years after the Emancipation Proclamation freed people from enslavement in the United States. Through the years, the NAACP has drawn its membership and financial support from African Americans and from whites who support the cause of civil rights. The NAACP has worked through the courts and the U.S. Congress to gain full citizenship for African Americans. The organization brought lynching to a halt. It has also helped to abolish forced segregation and continues to work for equal education and employment. Today, the NAACP has 650,000 members.*

AFTER YOU READ

EXPLORING YOUR RESPONSES

1. When Chavis was 12 years old, his father gave him a membership card to the NAACP. How does membership in an organization help people get involved with ideas and causes?

2. Chavis led a one-child protest to open Oxford's libraries to all people. Would you have become involved in this protest? Why?

3. A meeting with Dr. Martin Luther King, Jr., encouraged Chavis to become a student activist. Describe a person who has influenced you.

4. When he was released from jail, Chavis was not bitter about being falsely imprisoned. How might you have reacted?

5. Chavis is involved in helping young people who belong to gangs. What do you think Chavis can do to help them?

UNDERSTANDING WORDS IN CONTEXT

Read the following sentences from the biography. Think about what each underlined word means. In your notebook, write what the word means as it is used in the sentence.

1. Chavis . . . remembers feeling that being given that card was "part of my initiation into manhood."

2. Chavis's actions grew out of a proud family heritage of commitment to education and justice.

3. Chavis rallied students to work with civil rights organizations on behalf of municipal workers in several Southern cities. Many of these employees were sanitation workers who earned lower wages and had poorer working conditions than white municipal workers.

4. Despite having endured many hardships while in prison, Chavis refused to be <u>bitter</u>.

5. In this position, Chavis headed the first national environmental <u>summit</u> for people of color. The event brought together more than 800 leaders from the African American, Latino, Asian, and Native American communities.

RECALLING DETAILS

1. How were the Oxford libraries for African Americans and for whites different?

2. Why was John Chavis beaten to death by a mob in 1845?

3. Describe Ben Chavis's work as a student activist.

4. What was the Wilmington Ten Case?

5. How did time in prison affect Chavis's commitment to civil rights?

UNDERSTANDING INFERENCES

In your notebook, write two or three sentences from the biography that support each of the following inferences.

1. Chavis was influenced by his family's heritage.

2. Chavis became aware of discrimination at a young age.

3. Chavis is not afraid to stand up for what he believes in.

4. Chavis's time in prison only deepened his commitment to the causes he believes in.

5. Chavis wants the NAACP to address the problems of people of all cultures.

INTERPRETING WHAT YOU HAVE READ

1. How did Chavis's father influence his career?

2. Do you think Chavis's family supported his protest against segregated libraries in Oxford? Explain.

3. Why do you think Chavis's meeting with Dr. Martin Luther King, Jr., changed his life?

4. How was Chavis affected by his imprisonment in Wilmington?

5. Why do you think the NAACP selected Chavis to be its director?

ANALYZING QUOTATIONS

Read the following quotation from the biography and answer the questions below.

> *"One of the things I learned from Dr. Martin Luther King, Jr., is that there is no room for bitterness. You can't take that baggage around with you."*

1. According to Chavis, why is it not useful to remain bitter?

2. What events in Chavis's life show that he is not bitter?

3. How could bitterness affect a person's life?

THINKING CRITICALLY

1. Do you think Chavis's life would have been different without a strong family commitment to civil rights? Explain.

2. Why do you think Chavis decided to protest segregated libraries in Oxford?

3. Were Chavis's protest methods effective? Support your answer with information from his biography.

4. Chavis was influenced by Dr. Martin Luther King, Jr. What similarities do you see between these two men?

5. Chavis has begun working with gang members. How is this an outgrowth of his beliefs?

JOHN JOHNSON

Although he is now the owner and publisher of *Ebony, Jet*, and other magazines, John Johnson began his life in poverty. Johnson believes that to overcome poverty, people need to set reachable goals. Accomplishing small goals allows them to gain confidence to move on to larger goals.

John Johnson is not a movie star, entertainer, athlete, or politician. Yet he is known and respected by celebrities. One of the richest men in the United States, Johnson is the owner of *Ebony* magazine. However, he did not start his life in luxury. Johnson and his mother were once welfare recipients,[1] and his schoolmates made fun of his ragged clothes. His rise from poverty is one of the great success stories of the century.

Johnson was born in Arkansas City, Arkansas, in January of 1918. When he was 8 years old, his father was killed in a sawmill accident. His mother, who had only a third-grade education, barely made ends meet. In 1927, when Johnson was nine, he and his mother, like hundreds of thousands of other Arkansas City residents, had to run for their lives when the Mississippi River flooded seven states.

The Johnsons lived for six weeks on high ground with their stranded[2] neighbors. When the water receded, they searched for their shack. At first they could not find it, and they were relieved. The government was paying to rebuild destroyed houses. As they were about to abandon[3] their search, bad luck struck again. The Johnsons' house—now battered and full of water and snakes—had been swept three blocks away but remained standing. They cleaned up the shack and started over again. While others around them despaired,[4] they took heart in the belief that "There's an advantage in every disadvantage, and a gift in every problem."

The gift that Johnson found in this problem was a lesson. After the flood, he saw that the people who had the hardest time

1. **recipients** (rih-SIHP-ee-uhnts) *n. pl.* those who are given something
2. **stranded** (STRAN-duhd) *adj.* left in a helpless position
3. **abandon** (uh-BAN-duhn) *v.* give up completely
4. **despaired** (dih-SPAIRD) *v.* lost all hope

were the poor. Wealthy people—including rich African Americans—quickly rebuilt. Johnson realized that wealthy people had more control over their lives than poor people did.

From that day on, Johnson's goal was to make a more secure life for himself, which included a comfortable home. "Men and women are limited not by the place of their birth, not by the color of their skin, but by the size of their hope," he has written.

When he was 15, in 1933, Johnson left Arkansas behind. His mother, who had remarried, used her savings to buy train tickets to Chicago, where there were better public schools for African American children. For a time, her husband remained in Arkansas.

Johnson and his mother found Chicago to be a city filled with struggling people. Many, like the Johnsons, relied on welfare, which was then called "relief." Instead of money, people on relief were given food, such as meat, beans, flour and salt.

Johnson says that over the years he has heard many people criticize the welfare system. Yet he feels that most of those comments come from people who are unfamiliar with poverty. "I've been there, and I have no hesitancy in saying that I'm in favor of welfare for those who need it. I certainly don't condemn it. When we were on welfare, we needed it." At the same time, he says that he succeeded not because his family was on welfare, but because they never lost the will to "end dependence on welfare." Relying too much on government help, he believes, can destroy a person's drive to achieve.

After two years, Johnson's stepfather joined the family in Chicago and found work. Johnson also helped out, earning money from part-time jobs. In his spare time, he strolled through streets dominated by the office buildings of Chicago's African American business leaders. In this way, he reminded himself of his own goal to succeed.

Even with his stepfather's help, life was not easy. Johnson's new school had a student population of 3,000—more than all the people in Arkansas City. Johnson was one of the poorest students. Even worse, his classmates laughed at his unsophisticated speech and clothes. Once again, he searched for an advantage and found it. That advantage, he decided, was *not* being wealthy, like some of his African American schoolmates. One of them was driven to school by a chauffeur.[5] Walking to school in his threadbare clothes on the coldest days, Johnson reasoned that his own poverty made him work harder. "It's not satisfaction but dissatisfaction that drives people to the heights. I was goaded, I was driven by the whip of social disapproval."

At home, he read self-improvement books, learning that he had the power to accomplish his goals. One book suggested that he practice talking in front of a mirror. He did, and forced himself to speak in class. "They laughed at me at first but they soon started applauding—because I was making sense and because I was speaking better than anyone else."

He spoke so well that he was eventually elected class president, and was invited to join a luncheon of outstanding high school students. It was at this luncheon that he met Harry Pace, an African American businessman.

Pace, who was the president of Supreme Liberty Life Insurance Company in Chicago, told Johnson that he had heard good reports about him. Pace offered Johnson part-time work that would pay his college fees. It was a meeting that changed Johnson's life. Before he started his first day at work, he studied Pace's company. "I was only 18 years old, but I already knew that you *never* go into a [person's] office unless you know more about him, about his background, his interests, his hobbies . . . than he knows about you."

While attending the University of Chicago, Johnson worked his way up through Supreme Life, eventually leaving college to become a full-time editor of the company newsletter. In this position, he used his spare minutes to study the history of African Americans in business. Johnson knew he wanted to go into business, but he wondered which service or product he should sell. (See **Did You Know?** on page 213 for more information about African Americans in business.)

---

5. **chauffeur** (SHOH-fuhr) *n.* a person hired to drive an automobile for others

When opportunity knocked, again he was ready. Pace was too busy to read many newspapers. He asked Johnson to collect stories from black-owned newspapers, and tell him about good and bad events concerning African Americans. "I started telling my friends about the amazing things I'd read. And I was usually the center of attention at social gatherings. . . . The response was almost always the same: 'Where can I find that article?' Some people said that they would pay me if I would let them know where this or that article appeared."

He now knew that he wanted to start a magazine to make these articles available to a larger audience. But he needed money. Most of the people he contacted thought that a magazine about African Americans would not be profitable. "For almost two months, week after week, I went from office to office in Black Chicago and was told no." Johnson turned to his mother. She had no cash, but she took out a $500 loan on her new furniture. It was enough to get her son's magazine, *Negro Digest*, started in 1942.

The problem then was getting the magazine placed on newsstands throughout the city. Distributors[6] would not handle African American magazines. That did not stop Johnson. He visited the owner of the biggest magazine distribution company, listening politely as this man explained that his company could not deliver *Negro Digest* to newsstands because "colored books don't sell." Johnson did not lose his temper. Instead, he left his business card.

Back in his office, Johnson called 30 of his friends, asking them to go to various newsstands and demand *Negro Digest*. The tactic worked. The distributor believed that he had misjudged the potential market for an African American news magazine. He called Johnson and said that he had changed his mind.

Negro Digest was a hit from the start. By the age of 31, Johnson had earned a million dollars. But he continued to confront racial roadblocks in the business world. The more

6. **distributors** (dihs-TRIHB-yuht-uhrz) *n. pl.* people who deliver a product over a large area

successful Johnson grew in business, the more complications he encountered. In 1945, Johnson used the profits from *Negro Digest* to launch *Ebony*, a magazine that added pictures to information and news. The first 25,000 copies of *Ebony* sold out in hours. A year later, the magazine, now in color, was selling 275,000 copies monthly. *Ebony*'s appeal seemed to be not only its focus on the news, but on the more positive aspects of African American life, including the success stories of athletes, business people, entertainers, and people from all walks of life.

To meet the demand for his product, Johnson opened *Ebony* offices around the country. However, many white building owners refused to rent him office space. Although Johnson needed advertising from major corporations for the continued growth of his publication, white corporate managers refused to advertise in his magazine.

Johnson met each challenge, and eventually opened offices in many major cities. He also developed a large sales force. Today, nine million people read *Ebony*. It can be found on most newsstands in the United States as well as in foreign cities.

Johnson feels that in business it is important not to focus on what you need, but on what others need. He says that he did not start his business to become rich, but to provide a service to others and to improve his life. He advises those starting out to "dream small dreams." Too large a dream can be discouraging, he says, while dreaming small means "every time you accomplish a small goal, it gives you confidence to go on from there."

Although *Negro Digest* is no longer published, his company owns not only *Ebony*, but also several other publications, including the pocket-sized African American news magazine *Jet*. He also owns many other companies involved in cosmetics, hair care, fashion, and book publishing. Johnson is worth an estimated $400 million. Although thousands of people work for him, he still makes all the big decisions—including who will appear on the covers of his magazines.

Johnson spends his days in meetings, brainstorming with managers. In the last three decades, he has met and talked with every president of the United States. Celebrities turn to him for advice on making sound business investments.

Married since 1941, Johnson and his wife, Eunice, adopted two children—a son, John Johnson, Jr., and a daughter, Linda. His wife is the director of *Ebony*'s traveling fashion show. His daughter is the president of *Ebony*. Unfortunately, John, Jr., had sickle-cell anemia, a blood disease that primarily affects people of African descent. Symptoms include exhaustion, joint pain, and blood clots. He died in 1981, at the age of 25. His son's illness changed the way Johnson views his own life. He cut back on business trips and now spends more time with his family.

Today, Johnson owns several homes. One is on a hilltop in Palm Springs, California. Johnson enjoys the view. He advises youngsters to focus on a "vision that pulls you further than you want to go and forces you to use your hidden strengths." Even the worst setbacks in life can be advantages, he says. "What all men and women need is an irrevocable[7] act that forces you . . . to be the best that you can be."

> ***Did You Know?*** *Free African Americans have been operating businesses in the United States since before the Revolutionary War. In fact, George Washington's favorite pub, Fraunces' Tavern, in New York City, was owned by an African American, Samuel Fraunces. Other early African Americans owned building, insurance, barbering, tailoring, furniture-making, funeral, and restaurant businesses. Despite many nighttime raids, in which African American-owned establishments were burned down by white racists, African Americans continued to invest in businesses. Early in the 20th century, one of the wealthiest women in the United States was Madam C.J. Walker of Indianapolis, Indiana. She sold a line of hair care products.*

---

7. **irrevocable** (IH-rehv-uh-kuh-buhl) *adj.* unchangeable

AFTER YOU READ

EXPLORING YOUR RESPONSES

1. Johnson never gave up his goal. Tell about a time when you, or someone you know, displayed the same determination.

2. Johnson moved closer to his goal when his family moved to Chicago. How can moving from a small town to a big city change a person's life?

3. Johnson found something positive in the worst situations. How might you create exciting opportunities for yourself? Be specific.

4. Classmates teased Johnson about his speech and clothes. How might you have reacted to such a situation?

5. Imagine you could start a business of your own. What would that business be? Why do you think you would be good at it?

UNDERSTANDING WORDS IN CONTEXT

Read the following sentences from the biography. Think about what each underlined word means. In your notebook, write what the word means as it is used in the sentence.

1. Johnson and his mother were once welfare recipients, and his schoolmates made fun of his ragged clothes.

2. The Johnsons lived for six weeks on high ground with their stranded neighbors.

3. As they were about to abandon their search, bad luck struck again. The Johnsons' house . . . had been swept three blocks away but remained standing.

4. While others around them despaired, they took heart in the belief that "There's an advantage in every disadvantage, and a gift in every problem."

5. The problem then was getting the magazine placed on newsstands throughout the city. <u>Distributors</u> would not handle African American magazines.

RECALLING DETAILS

1. Why did Johnson move to Chicago?
2. How did walking through Chicago remind Johnson of his goal?
3. Why did Johnson improve his speech?
4. What led Johnson to believe that African Americans would buy a magazine that told about their lives?
5. How did Johnson convince a reluctant distributor to place his magazine on newsstands?

UNDERSTANDING INFERENCES

In your notebook, write two or three sentences from the biography that support each of the following inferences.

1. The flood helped Johnson shape his view of the future.
2. Johnson believes that people can work their way out of poverty.
3. Seeing wealthier boys convinced Johnson that he was, in some ways, better off than they were.
4. Working for an insurance company helped Johnson become a successful publisher.
5. Johnson's publications seemed to be just what people had been waiting for.

INTERPRETING WHAT YOU HAVE READ

1. Johnson started a magazine even though several businessmen warned him it would not be profitable. What does this tell you about how people become successful?

2. How do you think Johnson felt about using the money his mother borrowed on her furniture to start his company?

3. How do you think Johnson felt when the distributor told him that his company did not handle African American publications?

4. How might *Ebony* reflect Johnson's feelings about African Americans?

5. How did Johnson change over the years? How did he remain the same?

ANALYZING QUOTATIONS

Read the following quotation from the biography and answer the questions below.

> *"It's not satisfaction but dissatisfaction that drives people to the heights. I was goaded, I was driven by the whip of social disapproval."*

1. What do you think Johnson meant by saying that he "was driven by the whip of social disapproval"?

2. How could being satisfied with life be harmful?

3. Do you agree with Johnson's argument? Explain.

THINKING CRITICALLY

1. How did learning to communicate well help Johnson as a magazine publisher?

2. Do you agree that it is important to know the background of a person before you discuss business with him or her? Explain.

3. Why do you think distributors feared that a magazine about African Americans would not sell?

4. Why do you think Johnson launched *Ebony*?

5. Why do you think Johnson is successful in business?

MARIAN WRIGHT EDELMAN

Marian Wright Edelman, founder of the Children's Defense Fund, and Representative Patricia Schroeder talk with children at Shiloh Baptist Church's Child Care Center in Washington, D.C. Edelman founded CDF to solve problems she observed in her work with the NAACP Legal Defense and Education Fund in Mississippi.

As a young lawyer in Mississippi, Marian Wright Edelman tried to calm a group of angry teenagers during the dark hours that followed the assassination of Dr. Martin Luther King, Jr. One young man turned to her and asked why he should listen to her when he believed that he had no future.

In the years that followed, Edelman never forgot the teenager's frustration. Indeed, the exchange of words led her to become this country's leading advocate[1] for children's rights.

Marian was the youngest of Arthur and Margaret Wright's five children. She was born in 1939, in Bennettsville, South Carolina, a town that was typical of Southern towns at that time. The schools were racially segregated. African Americans also were prevented from enjoying many things that white citizens took for granted. They were not allowed to play in local parks or to sit down at lunch counters. They were not allowed to swim in the swimming pool that was across the street from the Wrights' home. The town's African American children had to swim in a dangerous creek. But discrimination could be more than painful. It could also be deadly. A childhood friend of Edelman's died because, as an African American child, he couldn't get the medical treatment he needed to save his life.

Fortunately, the Wright children were surrounded by a community of family, friends, neighbors, and teachers. Their support helped Marian develop self-respect and self-confidence. "They believed in us and we . . . believed in ourselves," she says.

One neighbor, whom the children and adults called Miz Amie, was a substitute grandmother for all the children—black and white—who played on the Wrights' block. "Miz Amie would sit on the third floor . . . and look down on everybody's kids. She never missed a beat about what anyone was doing."

---

1. **advocate** (AD-vuh-kuht) *n.* one who stands up for someone else

The Wrights provided and instilled[2] in their children a strong sense of caring and responsibility for others. Arthur Wright, a Baptist minister, and his wife, Margaret, started the first African American home for senior citizens in South Carolina. In addition to raising their own children, the Wrights took in 12 foster children. As a young girl, Edelman helped to cook and clean at the home for senior citizens. She was brought up believing that "service is the rent we pay for living." Pitching in and helping were important. "The only time my father wouldn't give me a chore was when I was reading, so I read a lot," she recalls.

Education was also important in the Wright home. Edelman's father, who died when she was 14, told his daughter to never "let anyone get between you and your education." After graduating from high school, she entered Spelman College in Atlanta, the largest college for African American women in the nation. During her junior year, she won a Merrill Scholarship to study in Europe. Her travels took her to Paris, Geneva, and Moscow. (See the biography of Johnnetta Cole on page 191 for more information about Spelman and other historically black colleges.)

Upon Edelman's return to Spelman, she saw that many changes had taken place. The time was the late 1950s, and the Civil Rights Movement was gaining momentum[3] in the South. Martin Luther King, Jr., and other civil rights leaders came to the campus to speak. They urged the students to protest segregation by organizing sit-ins at Atlanta's City Hall. When Edelman joined them, she was arrested along with hundreds of other students. She spent a night in jail.

Edelman entered Yale Law School in New Haven, Connecticut, in 1960, to study law because she wanted to help African Americans. Shortly before her graduation, three years later, she applied for a job with the National Association for the Advancement of Colored People (NAACP) Legal Defense and

---

2. **instilled** (ihn-STIHLD) *v.* taught or introduced a little at a time
3. **momentum** (moh-MEHNT-uhm) *n.* force or speed resulting from movement

Education Fund. This organization provides lawyers for people whose civil rights have been abused or denied.

Edelman chose to represent the Fund in Mississippi. She decided to go there because in the 1960s there were only three African American lawyers in a state of 900,000 African American residents. After her arrival in Mississippi during the summer of 1964, she quickly learned about the difficulty of her task.

Thousands of white and black students had poured into the state to work for the Mississippi Summer Project. As in many Southern states, African Americans were discouraged from voting in a variety of ways, including threats of injury or damage to their property. Her first case involved freeing hundreds of jailed college students who had been working on the movement to help African Americans vote.

Most of Edelman's clients, however, were African Americans who were pursuing their civil rights to help their children get a better education, or to find jobs that offered better pay and working conditions. Traveling around the Mississippi Delta, she became alarmed at the living conditions of the people she met. They were the poorest people she had ever seen in the United States. Even if she had been able to help them win the right to eat at a lunch counter, many would not be able to afford the price of the meal. Outraged at the poverty she saw, Edelman began requesting funds to help the poor improve their lives. She won a major victory by forcing the federal government to restore a Head Start educational program for preschoolers in Mississippi.

One of the people she met in Mississippi was Peter B. Edelman, her future husband. Edelman, who was also a lawyer, was an assistant to New York Senator Robert F. Kennedy. She had been asked to accompany Kennedy, Edelman, and members of a Senate subcommittee on a tour of the Delta region. They were there to see, firsthand, that some people in the United States were among the world's neediest. They toured shantytowns[4] in which people had little food for their children,

---

4. **shantytowns** (SHAN-tee-townz) *n. pl.* the section of a city in which there are many small, rundown homes

and no running water or electricity. Shaken, the group returned to Washington, D.C. The tour moved them to propose laws that would eliminate these conditions.

After a long-distance courtship between Mississippi and Washington, D.C., the Edelmans married in 1966, and Marian Wright Edelman moved to the nation's capital to be with her husband.

Edelman had many concerns about children in the United States. She remembered the boy who shouted that he had no future. She couldn't forget the babies in the Delta whose stomachs were swollen from hunger. She approached lawmakers in Congress to set aside money or to change laws that would improve the lives of millions of children of all races throughout the country. (See **Did You Know?** on page 222 for more information about Catherine Ferguson, a 19th-century African American child advocate.)

In 1973, Edelman started the Children's Defense Fund (CDF) to deal with the problems of youth unemployment, homelessness, child abuse, teen pregnancy, the scarcity[5] of medical care, and other issues. Today, she has a staff of 100 at the group's Washington, D.C., headquarters and a budget of $10.5 million.

Edelman is widely admired for her work on behalf of children, but she and the CDF have their critics. Some lawmakers say that her views about using government money to solve social problems are out of step with the 1990s. But Edelman notes that government dollars feed and inoculate poor children and provide support systems for children and their families.

In 1992, Edelman wrote a national bestseller, *The Measure of Our Success: A Letter to My Children and Yours*. The book began as a letter to her three grown sons. The letter contains "25 Lessons for Life." Three of Edelman's lessons are:

- "Never work just for money or power. They won't save your soul or build a decent family to help you sleep at night."

- "Remember your roots, your history, and the forebears' shoulders on which you stand."

5. **scarcity** (SKER-suht-ee) *n.* inadequate supply

- "Be confident that you can make a difference."

The last lesson is one that Marian Wright Edelman has put into practice throughout her life.

> ***Did You Know?*** *One of the earliest people to work on behalf of children in the United States was Catherine Ferguson, a former slave. Ferguson was born in 1774, aboard a ship bound for New York. When she was 8 years old, her mother was sold to another owner and Ferguson never saw her again. She later bought her freedom with the help of some white friends. As a free woman, Ferguson started an integrated Sunday school for 48 African American and white poor, homeless children. A minister in New York City allowed her to set up her school in the basement of his church, and provided teaching assistants. For the next 40 years, Ferguson supervised the education and well-being of the city's poor children. Her school, the Murray Street Sabbath School, was the first Sunday school in the United States.*

AFTER YOU READ

EXPLORING YOUR RESPONSES

1. Her family and community helped Edelman develop self-respect and self-confidence. How can families and communities help children develop these qualities?

2. Edelman's father believed in the importance of education. What do you think education can do for you?

3. Edelman decided to become a lawyer because she wanted to represent African Americans. What career might you choose that would help others?

4. During the Civil Rights Movement, thousands of students demonstrated against segregation. Do you think that students today would protest something they felt was wrong? Explain.

5. Edelman never forgot the young man who felt he had no future. What would you say to someone your age who felt the same way?

UNDERSTANDING WORDS IN CONTEXT

Read the following sentences from the biography. Think about what each underlined word means. In your notebook, write what the word means as it is used in the sentence.

1. Edelman never forgot the teenager's frustration. Indeed, this exchange of words led her to become this country's leading advocate for children's rights.

2. The Wrights provided and instilled in their children a strong sense of caring and responsibility for others.

3. The time was the late 1950s, and the Civil Rights Movement was gaining momentum in the South.

4. They toured shantytowns in which people had little food for their children, and no running water or electricity.

5. Edelman started the Children's Defense Fund (CDF) to deal with the problems of youth unemployment, homelessness, child abuse, teen pregnancy, the <u>scarcity</u> of medical care, and other issues.

RECALLING DETAILS

1. What event led Edelman to become an advocate for children's rights?
2. How was Bennettsville, South Carolina, a typical Southern town in 1939?
3. How did Edelman's parents show they believed that "service is the rent we pay for living"?
4. Why did Edelman choose to study law?
5. Which problems did Edelman want to address when she started the Children's Defense Fund in 1973?

UNDERSTANDING INFERENCES

In your notebook, write two or three sentences from the biography that support each of the following inferences.

1. Edelman's childhood had an effect on her career choice.
2. The African American residents of Mississippi in the 1960s needed help in exercising their rights.
3. Edelman has been a successful advocate for children's rights.
4. Edelman is passing the lessons she learned on to her sons.
5. Edelman believes that she can make a difference.

INTERPRETING WHAT YOU HAVE READ

1. Why do you think African Americans were discouraged from voting?
2. Why do you think Edelman participated in the sit-ins, even though it meant going to jail?

3. Why didn't the U.S. Senators know about the conditions in the Mississippi Delta?

4. How did Edelman's move from Mississippi to Washington, D.C., change her work?

5. Edelman's bestseller is titled *The Measure of Our Success*. How do you think Edelman measures success?

ANALYZING QUOTATIONS

Read the following quotation from the biography and answer the questions below.

> *"Never work just for money or power. They won't save your soul or build a decent family to help you sleep at night."*

1. What do you think Edelman means by this statement?

2. How has Edelman shown that she believes this statement?

3. If you could restate this belief in your own words, what would you say?

THINKING CRITICALLY

1. In what ways might Edelman's career have been different if her parents had not been supportive?

2. Edelman wants her sons to "remember [their] roots, [their] history, and the forebears' shoulders on which [they] stand." Do you agree or disagree with this belief? Why?

3. Imagine that you are an adult with children. What three lessons for life would you want them to remember?

4. Do you agree that the government should provide help for children in need? Why?

5. Edelman started the CDF to help children and teenagers. What issues do you think are most important to teenagers?

CULTURAL CONNECTIONS

Thinking About What People Do

1. Imagine you are one of the people in this unit. Write three journal entries describing "your" experiences and thoughts on three different days. Include details about "your" work.

2. Pretend that two of the people in this unit are meeting for the first time. With a partner, write a short dialogue in which the people describe to each other the issues that are important to them and the ways in which they support these issues.

3. With a partner, create a collage that shows what one of the people in this unit has accomplished. Use pictures from magazines and other available sources, or draw your own illustrations of the person's accomplishments. Finally, present your collage to the class.

Thinking About Culture

1. How did the African American cultural background of the subjects in this unit affect their choice of career? Choose one person, and use details from his or her biography to support your conclusions.

2. How were some of the people in this unit influenced by their families as they grew up or chose their life's work? Give three examples.

3. Compare the educational backgrounds of two people in this unit. What effects did their cultural backgrounds have on their education?

Building Research Skills

Work with a partner to complete the following activity.

Choose two of the people discussed in this unit who you think have similar character traits. Prepare a list of questions about their similarities and differences. Your questions might include:

Hint: The Bibliography at the back of this book lists articles and books to help you begin your research.

☆ What experiences have the two people shared?

☆ What differences do you see between them?

Hint: Remember to support your ideas with examples from the biographies and from your research.

☆ How were they influenced by their cultural heritage?

☆ How were their childhoods similar and different?

☆ How are their careers similar and different?

Next, go to the library to do research on the people you have chosen.

Hint: Make a Venn diagram to help you see similarities and differences between your subjects.

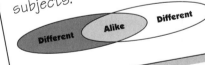

Write a short essay in which you compare and contrast the two people you have researched. Use your list of questions to help guide your writing. You might also use your Venn diagram to help you organize your essay.

Then present your essay orally to the class. If possible, display pictures of your subjects at home or at work.

Extending Your Studies

SOCIAL STUDIES **Your task:** *To give a two-minute oral presentation about a civic leader whose work you admire.* In this unit, you have read about several people who work in public service. These people have helped protect the rights of everyone. Think of another person whose public service you admire. This person could be a government leader, a spokesperson for a cause, or a local activist. Go to the library to find out more about that person. You might begin by answering these questions:

☆ With what issue is this person most concerned?

☆ How did this person become involved in the issue?

☆ What is the exact nature of the work this person does?

Once you have answered these and other questions, prepare a two-minute oral presentation. You might begin by telling why you admire this person. Organize the rest of the presentation chronologically—according to when significant events occurred in this person's life. If possible, show the class one or more pictures of the person involved in his or her work.

VISUAL ARTS **Your task:** *To create a pictorial color magazine.* John Johnson made his fortune by creating the magazines *Negro Digest* and *Ebony*. In groups of four or five, create pictorial magazines that you think your classmates would enjoy looking at and reading. First, look at popular magazines such as *Ebony, Life, Look,* and *Sports Illustrated* for ideas.

Next, choose a subject for your magazine. You may want to consider subjects dealing with the environment, a sport you enjoy, or a popular hobby. Then go to the library to find out what is new and interesting in that field. Each member of your group should write one or two short articles for the magazine.

Illustrations are very important in pictorial magazines. Each member of your group should contribute some art for your magazine. You may use original drawings or photographs, or copy illustrations from other sources. If you have access to a computer, you may want to include clip art or create some original computer art.

Finally, give your magazine a catchy name. Type, copy, assemble, and distribute the magazine to your classmates.

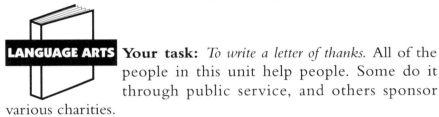 **Your task:** *To write a letter of thanks.* All of the people in this unit help people. Some do it through public service, and others sponsor various charities.

Imagine that you and your family have directly benefited from the work of one of the people in this unit. Write a thank-you note to that person.

Use the business letter format shown below. In the body of the letter, be sure to mention the ways the person has helped you.

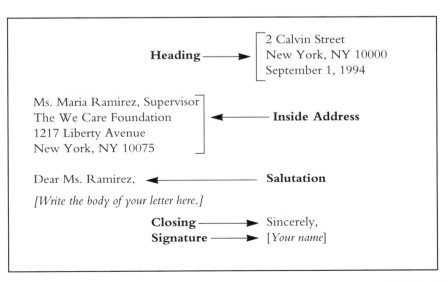

WRITING WORKSHOP

In Units 2 and 3, you wrote biographical sketches of a friend, and a family or community member. The information for these sketches came from memory or interviews. For this sketch, you will use books, magazines, and other sources to write a **researched biography.**

PREWRITING

Your first step will be to choose your subject. Whom have you read or heard about that interests you? Use the **prewriting** strategies you learned in Units 1–3, or try one of these ideas to get started.

Ask questions: Think about what you want to learn about particular fields. For example, imagine that you have read a magazine article about historically black colleges, like Spelman. You found the article fascinating, but you know very little about the organization and its history. List questions about the group and the people in it.

Another approach would be to start with people. For instance, you might list questions about African Americans you have read about in newspapers or in this book.

Finally, you might go to the library and look through magazines and books for ideas. List the people who catch your attention. Then narrow your focus to one person you feel is noteworthy, and for whom there are enough source materials. Here are some guidelines for your research.

Limit your topic: Concentrate on one or two turning points and significant events. Don't try to cover the person's entire life.

Locate your sources: Use the card catalog or computer in your library to locate books on your subject. Look for your subject's last name, and note the titles you find and their call numbers. For example:

Author	Title	Call Number
Rowan, Carl T.	*Breaking Barriers: A Memoir*	070.92 ROW

You will want to explore these library resources, too:

☆ The *Readers' Guide to Periodical Literature:* magazine articles on many subjects

☆ Other indexes: *The New York Times Index, Art Index,* and *Science and Technology Index,* among others

☆ Dictionaries and encyclopedias: specialized references, such as *Current Biography, American Women Writers, Contemporary Black Biographies, Notable Black American Women,* and *Dictionary of American Negro Biography*

Take notes: As you read, take notes on 3 x 5 note cards. On each card, write the title, author, publisher, date of publication, and page number of the book or magazine you use. Write your notes in your own words. If you want to quote someone, copy the words exactly and be sure to use quotation marks.

Organize your notes: First, arrange your notes in categories. Some categories might include Early Life, School Days, or People Who Influenced My Subject. Decide which information you will keep and what you will leave out. Focus on your purpose: What do you want your readers to learn about the person? Check all facts and figures.

Second, organize your ideas in a logical order. Chronological, or time, order can help you tell your story in a way your reader can easily understand.

Finally, decide on an interesting way to start your biography. You could catch your reader's interest by beginning with a quote from your subject, an important event in the person's life, or an intriguing question.

DRAFTING

Now that you have organized your notes, **draft** your biography. Remember that you need not worry about making it perfect. Just get your ideas down on paper. You will check for word usage and spelling errors later. Include a bibliography of all the sources you used.

Include a bibliography: At the end of your biography, list the materials you used, in alphabetical order. Use the following form:

Books:

Author	Title	City Published	Publisher	Copyright Date
Smith, Charles.	Alberta Grace.	New York:	Overland Press,	1992.

Magazines:

Author	Article Title	Magazine Title	Date	Page Numbers
Field, Renee.	"Dispensing Hope."	Lives Today.	30 April 1991:	55–57.

REVISING

Put your biography aside for a day or two. Then, with the help of another student who will act as your editor, evaluate and **revise** your work. See the directions for writers and student editors below.

Directions for Writers: Read your work aloud, listening to how it flows. Then ask yourself these questions:

☆ Does my opening hold my reader's attention?

☆ Are the ideas presented in a logical order?

☆ Did I include quotes from the subject?

☆ Does my writing focus on turning points?

Make notes for your next draft or revise your work before you give it to a student editor. Then ask the student editor to read your work. Listen carefully to his or her suggestions. If they seem helpful, use them to improve your writing when you revise your work.

Directions for Student Editors: Read the work carefully and respectfully, remembering that your purpose is to help the writer do his or her best work. Keep in mind that an editor should always make positive, helpful comments that point to specific parts of the essay. After you have read the work, use the following questions to help you direct your comments:

☆ What do I like most about the biography?

☆ Is the writing clear and logical?

☆ Do the subject's achievements and character come through?

☆ Has the writer used vivid details to describe the subject?

☆ Does the writer reveal why this person is noteworthy?

☆ What would I like to know more about?

PROOFREADING

When you are satisfied that your work says what you want it to say, **proofread** it for errors in spelling, punctuation, capitalization, and grammar. Then make a neat, final copy of your biographical essay.

PUBLISHING

After you have revised your writing, you are ready to **publish**, or share, it. Create a class book of Special People, Special Achievements. Form small groups to handle various bookmaking tasks. These tasks include:

☆ designing and creating a cover jacket

☆ organizing the book into several chapters

☆ writing the title page, contents page, and an introduction to the book

Then bind the biographies to make a book. After everyone in the class has had a chance to read it, lend the book to the school library for others to read.

GLOSSARY

Vowel Sound	Symbol	Respelling
a as in *hat*	a	HAT
a as in *day, date, paid*	ay	DAY, DAYT, PAYD
vowels as in *far, on*	ah	FAHR, AHN
vowels as in *dare, air*	ai	DAIR, AIR
vowels as in *saw, call, pour*	aw	SAW, KAWL, PAWR
e as in *pet, debt*	eh	PEHT, DEHT
e as in *seat, chief*; **y** as in *beauty*	ee	SEET, CHEEF, BYOO-tee
vowels as in *learn, fur, sir*	er	LERN, FER, SER
i as in *sit, bitter*; **ee** as in *been*	ih	SIHT, BIHT-uhr, BIHN
i as in *mile*; **y** as in *defy*; **ei** as in *height*	eye	MEYEL, dee-FEYE, HEYET
o as in *go*	oh	GOH
vowels as in *boil, toy*	oi	BOIL, TOI
vowels as in *foot, could*	o͝o	FO͝OT, KO͝OD
vowels as in *boot, rule, suit*	oo	BOOT, ROOL, SOOT
vowels as in *how, out, bough*	ow	HOW, OWT, BOW
vowels as in *up, come*	u	UP, KUM
vowels as in *use, use, few*	yoo	YOOZ, YOOS, FYOO
vowels in unaccented syllables (*schwas*) *again, upon, sanity*	uh	uh-GEHN, uh-PAHN, SAN-uh-tee

Consonant Sound	Symbol	Respelling
ch as in *choose, reach*	ch	CHOOZ, REECH
g as in *go, dig*	g	GOH, DIHG
gh as in *rough, laugh*	f	RUF, LAF

h as in *who, whole*	h	HOO, HOHL
j as in *jar*; **dg** as in *fudge*;		
g as in *gem*	j	JAHR, FUJ, JEHM
k as in *king*; **c** as in *come*;		
ch as in *Christmas*	k	KIHNG, KUM, KRIHS-muhs
ph as in *telephone*	f	TEHL-uh-fohn
s as in *treasure*; **g** as		
in *bourgeois*	zh	TREH-zhuhr, boor-ZHWAH
s as in *this, sir*	s	THIS, SEHR
sh as in *ship*	sh	SHIHP
th as in *thin*	th	THIHN
th as in *this*	<u>th</u>	<u>TH</u>IHS
wh as in *white*	wh	WHEYET
x as in *fix, axle*	ks	FIHKS, AK-suhl
x as in *exist*	gz	ihg-ZIHST
z as in *zero*; **s** as in *chasm*	z	ZEE-roh, KAZ-uhm

abandon (uh-BAN-duhn) *v.* give up completely, 208

accessible (ahk-SEHS-uh-buhl) *adj.* easy to understand, 7

activist (AK-tih-vuhst) *n.* one who takes direct action to achieve a goal, 201

administration (uhd-mihn-uh-STRAY-shuhn) *n.* the process of running an organization, 148

advocate (AD-vuh-kuht) *n.* one who stands up for someone else, 218

agenda (uh-JEHN-duh) *n.* a list or plan of things to do, 110

ancestors (AN-sehs-tuhrz) *n. pl.* people from whom one is descended, 194

anchor (ANG-kuhr) *n.* a person who introduces the stories of other television or radio journalists and remains in a fixed place, such as a studio, 55

apartheid (uh-PAHR-teyet) *n.* the former South African policy of strict racial segregation and discrimination against non-whites, 71

apprentice (uh-PREHN-tuhs) *adj.* one beginning to learn a trade or profession, 35

asserting (uh-SUHRT-ihng) *v.* stating one's position forcefully, 138

bastion (BAS-chuhn) *n.* a stronghold, 108

biases (BEYE-uhs-ihz) *n. pl.* unreasonable judgments; prejudices, 157

bitter (BIHT-uhr) *adj.* intensely unpleasant, 202

bizarre (bih-ZAHR) *adj.* extremely odd; unexpected, 25

boundaries (BOWN-dreez) *n. pl.* lines that separate areas, 147

boycott (BOI-kaht) *n.* a refusal to buy, sell, or use a product or service in order to express disapproval, 201

browse (BROWZ) *v.* to look casually, reading here and there, 8

chaplain (CHA-plihn) *n.* a person who conducts religious services, 52

chauffeur (SHOH-fuhr) *n.* a person hired to drive an automobile for others, 210

choreographed (KOHR-ee-uh-graft) *v.* arranged or directed a dancer's moves, 82

civil servant (SIH-vuhl SUHR-vuhnt) a person who works as a government employee, 90

commentator (KAHM-uhn-tayt-uhr) *n.* a person who reports, analyzes, and evaluates news events or trends, 19

conjure (KAHN-juhr) *v.* to call up as if by magic; to create, 36

conscience (KAHN-shuhns) *n.* a knowledge or sense of right and wrong, 73

conscious (KAHN-shuhs) *adj.* being aware; concerned, 90

consecutive (kuhn-SEHK-yuh-tihv) *adj.* following one after another, 18

contemporary (kuhn-TEHM-puh-rehr-ee) *adj.* modern; having to do with today, 101

cramming (KRAM-ihng) *v.* to study for an exam in a hurried, intensive way, 130

credentials (crih-DEHN-shuhlz) *n. pl.* diplomas or other certificates that show evidence of ability, 147

crucial (KROO-shuhl) *adj.* extremely important; essential, 45

customs (KUHS-tuhmz) *n. pl.* ways of behaving that are passed down from one generation to the next, 194

despaired (dih-SPAIRD) *v.* lost all hope, 208

devices (dih-VEYES-uhz) *n. pl.* techniques; methods to achieve an artistic result, 100

diplomacy (dih-PLOH-muh-cee) *n.* skill in dealing with people, 149

discards (DIHS-kahrdz) *n. pl.* unwanted items, 53

dismantled (dihs-MAN-tuhld) v. took apart, 155

distributors (dihs-TRIHB-yuht-uhrz) *n. pl.* people who deliver a product over a large area, 211

divert (duh-VERT) *v.* to distract someone, 109

documentary (dahk-yuh-MEHNT-uh-ree) *adj.* based on facts, 99

domestic (duh-MEHS-tihk) *n.* a household servant, 90

dormitory (DAWR-muh-tawr-ee) *n.* a building that houses students, 149

ecstasy (EHK-stuh-see) *n.* great delight, 8

embittered (ihm-BIHT-uhrd) *adj.* made resentful or angry, 46

emeritus (ih-MEHR-uht-uhs) *adj.* holding an honorary title after retirement, 92

entices (ihn-TEYES-uhs) *v.* attracts artfully, 28

envoy (EHN-voy) *n.* a person sent by a government or ruler to transact diplomatic business, 19

epilepsy (EHP-uh-lehp-see) *n.* a physical disorder marked by convulsions, 131

epithets (EH-puh-thehts) *n. pl.* insulting names, 52

equivalent (ih-KWIHV-uh-luhnt) *adj.* equal, 166

eradicate (ih-RA-duh-kayt) *v.* eliminate; do away with, 186

eventually (ih-VEHN-choo-wuhl-ee) *adj.* finally; in the end, 164

exploitation (ehks-ploi-TAY-shuhn) *n.* to make immoral use of something for profit, 72

exploits (EHK-sploits) *n. pl.* deeds; acts, 186

extras (EHK-struhs) *n. pl.* people hired to act in a group scene in a motion picture, 71

faculty (FAK-uhl-tee) *n.* all of the teachers or professors at a school, 36

fazed (FAYZD) *v.* disturbed; stopped, 82

franchise (FRAN-cheyez) *n.* a license to sell products in a certain area, 187

fundamentally (fun-duh-MEHNT-tuh-lee) *adj.* basically; essentially, 195

gangly (GAN-glee) *adj.* loosely and awkwardly built, 83

garnered (GAHR-nuhrd) *v.* earned; collected, 45

hallowed (HAL-ohd) *adj.* sacred; greatly respected, 186

heft (HEHFT) *n.* heaviness; weight, 8

hemispherectomy (hehm-uh-sfeer-EHK-tuh-mee) *n.* surgical removal of one half of the brain, 131

heritage (HEHR-uht-ihj) *n.* something that is handed down from one's ancestors, 200

honors (AH-nuhrz) *n. pl.* awards in recognition of academic achievement, 26

idolized (EYED-uhl-eyezd) *v.* worshipped, 84

inducted (ihn-DUKT-uhd) *v.* admitted as a member, 186

initiation (ih-nihsh-ee-AY-shuhn) *n.* admittance to a club or group with a special ceremony, 200

inkling (IHNK-lihng) *n.* hint; clue, 9

innovative (IHN-uh-vay-tihv) *adj.* something new or changed, 195

insights (ihn-SEYETZ) *n. pl.* clear understanding, 19

inspiration (ihn-spuh-RAY-shun) *n.* action or power that moves the intellect or emotions, 43

instilled (ihn-STIHLD) *v.* taught or introduced a little at a time, 219

integrity (ihn-TEHG-ruht-ee) *n.* a code of high moral or artistic values, 72

intensive (ihn-TEN-sihv) *adj.* highly concentrated, 139

intention (ihn-TEHN-shuhn) *n.* determination to act in a certain way, 71

intern (IHN-tuhrn) *n.* a doctor who is serving an apprenticeship as an assistant resident in a hospital, 130

internship (IHN-tuhrn-shihp) *n.* a job, paid or unpaid, that allows a student to get experience working in a profession, 99

intimate (IHN-tuh-muht) *adj.* familiar; well-acquainted, 8

irrevocable (IH-rehv-uh-kuh-buhl) *adj.* unchangeable, 213

laureate (LAWR-ee-iht) *n.* a person who is honored for achievement, 7

legendary (LEHJ-uhn-dehr-ee) *adj.* relating to a legend; famous, 81

liberated (LIHB-uh-ray-tuhd) *v.* set free, 194

lucrative (LOO-kruh-tihv) *adj.* producing wealth, 185

lyrical (LEER-uh-kuhl) *adj.* like a song, 27

mainstream (MAYN-streem) *adj.* related to the dominant culture, 100

maturity (muh-TOOR-uht-ee) *n.* being older and having wisdom, 184

mechanisms (MEHK-uh-nihz-uhmz) *n. pl.* processes; systems for doing something, 99

medium (MEE-dee-uhm) *n.* a means of communicating to the general public, such as newspapers, radio, TV, and movies, 108

mentor (MEHN-tawr) *n.* a trusted counselor or guide, 91

missionaries (MIHSH-uhn-air-eez) *n. pl.* people who are sent to another culture to perform a special duty, 128

mobile (MOH-buhl) *adj.* able to move or advance in social status, 9

momentum (moh-MEHNT-uhm) *n.* force or speed resulting from movement, 219

municipal (myoo-NIHS-uh-puhl) *adj.* relating to local government, 201

nautical (NAWT-ih-kuhl) *adj.* having to do with the sea and ships, 37

negotiate (nih-GOH-shee-ayt) *v.* discuss or bargain to reach an agreement, 19

neurosurgery (NOOR-oh-suhr-juh-ree) *n.* surgery on the brain or spinal cord, 127

notion (NOH-shuhn) *n.* a theory or belief, 53

obscure (ahb-SKYOOR) *adj.* relatively unknown, 185

offensive (uh-FEHN-sihv) *adj.* giving painful or unpleasant sensations, 72

pallet (PAH-liht) *n.* a small bed or pad filled with straw, 16

Pentecostal (pehnt-ih-KAWS-tuhl) *n.* form of Christian faith that emphasizes revivalist worship, 71

perceptions (puhr-SEHP-shuhnz) *n. pl.* beliefs; mental images, 80

persuaded (puhr-SWAYD-uhd) *v.* caused to do or believe something by argument; convinced, 149

philosopher (fuh-LAH-suh-fuhr) *n.* a person who tries to answer questions about the meaning of life, 35

pigment (PIHG-muhnt) *n.* a coloring matter in plants and animals, 147

pinnacle (PIH-nih-kuhl) *n.* the highest point, 83

plaque (PLAK) *n.* a thin piece of metal that honors a person, 184

playwrights (PLAY-reyets) *n. pl.* people who write dramas to be perfomed on stage, 43

ploy (PLOI) *n.* a tactic used to frustrate an opponent, 54

pluralistic (ploor-uh-LIHS-tihk) *adj.* having to do with different groups, 100

preceded (prih-SEED-uhd) *v.* went before, 111

prejudice (PREH-juh-duhs) *n.* a negative opinion that has been formed without information, 27

premier (prih-MIHR) *adj.* first in position or rank, 157

prestigious (preh-STIHJ-uhs) *adj.* highly honored or respected, 92

profusely (pruh-FYOOS-lee) *adj.* pouring forth in great quantities, 127

prominent (PRAHM-uh-nehnt) *adj.* well-known; important, 192

provocative (pruh-VAHK-uht-ihv) *adj.* intending to excite or provoke, 98

rangy (RAYN-jee) *adj.* slender and long-limbed, 82

raves (RAYVZ) *n. pl.* favorable criticism, 92

recipients (rih-SIHP-ee-uhnts) *n. pl.* those who are given something, 208

reconciled (REHK-uhn-seyeld) *v.* became friendly again; brought into harmony, 109

regally (REE-guh-lee) *adv.* like a queen or king, 53

regional (REE-juhn-uhl) *adj.* local; in one part of the country, 45

register (REH-juh-stuhr) *v.* officially enter a name onto a record or list, 52

registrar (REHJ-uh-strahr) *n.* an official keeper of records, 164

reinforced (ree-uhn-FOHRST) *v.* strengthened, 137

required (rih-KWEYERD) *v.* took; needed, 148

reserved (rih-ZERVD) *adj.* quiet in speech and manner; self-restrained, 107

resident (REHZ-ih-duhnt) *n.* a person who is pursuing advanced medical or surgical training, 130

respectable (rih-SPEHK-tuh-buhl) *adj.* fairly large in size or amount; deserving esteem, 91

retort (rih-TAWRT) *n.* a quick, witty reply, 108

rigorous (RIHG-uh-ruhs) *adj.* very strict; demanding, 139

scarcity (SKER-suht-ee) *n.* inadequate supply, 221

scuttled (SKU-tuhld) *v.* destroyed; ruined, 34

selective (suh-LEHK-tihv) *adj.* choosing few out of many, 165

seminary (SEH-muh-ner-ee) *n.* an institution of higher education, often for studying to become a minister or priest, 54

serfs (SERFZ) *n. pl.* slaves; servants, 168

shantytowns (SHAN-tee-townz) *n. pl.* the section of a city in which there are many small, rundown homes, 220

sharecropper (SHAIR-krahpuhr) *n.* a farmer who works the landowner's farm for a share of the crops, 89

signature (SIHG-nuh-choor) *adj.* identified with a person, 82

sophisticated (suh-FIHS-tuh-kayt-uhd) *adj.* worldly-wise, 82

spheres (SFIHRS) *n.* areas, 141

stark (STAHRK) *adj.* plain; without ornament, 98

stereotypical (stehr-ee-uh-TIHP-ihk-uhl) *adj.* not original or individual, 73

stows (STOHZ) *v.* hides in a ship or airplane to gain free travel, 37

stranded (STRAN-duhd) *adj.* left in a helpless position, 208

submitted (suhb-MIHT-uhd) *v.* presented to others for consideration, 45

summit (SUM-iht) *n.* a conference of high officials, 202

syndicated (SIHN-duh-kayt-uhd) *adj.* appearing in several publications at the same time, 19

tenacity (tuh-NAS-uht-ee) *n.* the quality of holding fast; persistence, 137

tolerant (TAH-luh-ruhnt) *adj.* willing to respect or try to understand customs, ideas, or beliefs that are different from one's own, 155

transforming (trans-FAWHRM-ihng) *v.* changing the shape of something, 164

translated (tranz-LAYT-uhd) *v.* changed, turned into, 158

tutorials (too-TAWR-ee-uhlz) *n. pl.* individual lessons, 159

vulnerable (VUL-nuhr-uh-buhl) *adj.* open to damage, 10

wryly (REYE-lee) *adv.* in a cleverly humorous way, 37

BIBLIOGRAPHY

Auguste, Donna

Markoff, John. "Reprogramming the Hacker Elite." *The New York Times*, Jan. 2, 1994: p.6.

Carson, Benjamin

Carson, Ben, M.D., and Cecil Murphey. *Gifted Hands: The Ben Carson Story*. Grand Rapids, MI: Zondervan, 1990.

Chavis, Benjamin

Ellis, David. "Man in Motion." *People*, July 19, 1993: pp. 65–66.

Normant, Lynn. "Ben Chavis: A New Director, A New Direction at the NAACP." *Ebony*, July 1993: pp. 76-80.

Cobb, Jewel Plummer

Cobb, Jewel. "Filters for Women in Science." *Annals of the New York Academy of Sciences*, vol. 323: 1979.

Yount, Lisa. "Black Scientists." New York: Facts on File, 1991.

Cole, Johnnetta B.

Cleage, Page. "Johnnetta Cole." *Ms.*, November/December 1993: pp.42–44.

Cole, Johnnetta B. *Conversations: Straight Talk with America's Sister President*. New York: Doubleday, 1993.

Dove, Rita

Molotsky, Irvin. "Rita Dove Named Next Poet Laureate: First Black in Post." *The New York Times,* May 19, 1993: p. C15.

Streitfield, David. "Laureate for a New Age." *Washington Post*, May 19, 1993: p. 1.

Edelman, Marian Wright

Granant, Diane. "Mother Knows Best." *The Washingtonian*, Nov. 1992: pp. 41–45.

Viorst, Judith. "The Woman Behind the First Lady." *Redbook*, June 1993: pp.65–66.

Erving, Julius

Araton, Harvey. "Erving Still Soars Above the Rest." *The New York Times,* Feb. 10, 1993: p. B12.

Williams, Michael W., ed. *The African American Encyclopedia*, vol. 2. New York: Marshall Cavendish, 1993.

Hunter-Gault, Charlayne
Greener, Melissa Fay. "Things Were Never the Same Again." *The New York Times Book Review*, Nov. 22, 1992: p. 9.
Hunter-Gault, Charlayne. *In My Place*. New York: Vintage Books, 1992.
Jamison, Judith
Jamison, Judith. *Dancing Spirit*. New York: Doubleday, 1993.
Jemison, Mae
Current Biography Yearbook 1993. New York: H.W. Wilson Co., 1993: pp. 277-281.
Giovanni, Nikki. "Shooting for the Moon." *Essence*, April 1993: p. 58.
Johnson, Charles
Current Biography Yearbook 1991. New York: H.W. Wilson Co., 1991: pp. 310-314.
Williams, Marjorie. "The Author's Solo Passage." *Washington Post*, Dec. 4, 1990: p. D1.
Johnson, John
Bigelow, Barbara Carlisle, ed. *Contemporary Black Biography: Profiles from the International Black Community*, vol. 3. Detroit: Gale Research, Inc., 1993: p. 102.
Johnson, John H., with Lerone Bennett, Jr. *Succeeding Against the Odds: The Autobiography of a Great American Businessman*. New York: Amistad Press, 1989.
Lawrence, Jacob
Jacob Lawrence: The Migration Series, introductory essay, Gates, Henry Louis, Jr. Rappahannock Press in association with The Phillips Collection.
Halpin, James. "Jacob Lawrence at 70." *The Weekly: Seattle's Newsmagazine*, Oct. 7-Oct. 13, 1987: pp. 24-31.
MacClay, Catharine. "History in the Making." *San Jose Mercury News*, Arts & Books, Nov. 14, 1993: pp. 15-17.
Marsalis, Branford and Wynton
Moritz, Charles, ed. *Current Biography*. New York: H.W. Wilson Co., 1991: pp. 388-391. (Branford)
Moritz, Charles, ed. *Current Biography*. New York: H.W. Wilson

Co., 1994: pp. 255-257. (Wynton)

Segell, Michael. "Happy to Be Blue." *Cosmopolitan*, Apr. 1992: p. 96. (Wynton)

Watrous, Peter. "Here's Branford." *The New York Times Magazine*, May 3, 1992: pp. 40, 42, 72, 78.

Morrison, Toni

Gates, David. "Keep Your Eyes on the Prize." *Newsweek,* Oct. 18, 1993: p. 89.

Gray, Paul. "Rooms of Their Own." *Time,* Oct. 18, 1993: pp. 86-87.

Moses, Robert

Jetter, Alexis. "Mississippi Learning." *The New York Times Magazine,* Feb. 21, 1993: p 28.

Rowan, Carl

Bigelow, Barbara Carlisle, ed. *Contemporary Black Biography: Profiles from the International Black Community*, vol. 1. Detroit: Gale Research, Inc.,1993: pp. 208-211.

Rowan, Carl. *Breaking Barriers: A Memoir*. Boston, MA: Little, Brown and Company, 1991.

Simpson, Lorna

Jones, Kellie. "Lorna Simpson: Conceptual Artist." *Emerge*, Jan. 1991: p. 40.

Wallach, Amei. "Lorna Simpson: Right Time, Right Place." *New York Newsday,* Sept. 19, 1990: Part II, p. 8.

(Video) "For the Sake of the Viewer," Henry Art Gallery, University of Washington.

Washington, Denzel

Current Biography Yearbook 1992. New York: H.W. Wilson Co., 1992: pp. 592-596.

Williams, Lena. "Fighting Fire With Fire." *The New York Times Magazine*, Oct. 25, 1992: pp. 36-39, 64-67.

Wood, Joe. "X." *Rolling Stone*, Nov. 26, 1992: pp. 34-36, 39-40, 80-81.

Wilson, August

Current Biography Yearbook 1987. New York: H.W. Wilson Co., 1987: pp. 607-610.

Staples, Brent. "Spotlight on August Wilson." *Essence*, Aug. 1987: pp. 51, 111-112.

CAREER RESOURCES

Unit 1: Literature and Communications

These magazines present students' and adult writers' work, and articles that discuss the craft of writing.

The Horn Book (includes book reviews for young people)

Stone Soup (a literary magazine for young people)

Story (a literary magazine for advanced readers)

Writer's Digest (features articles about ways to improve writing, and interviews with writers)

Find out more about the poets, novelists, and thinkers of the Harlem Renaissance in this book:

Lewis, David L. *When Harlem Was in Vogue.* New York: Knopf, 1980.

Unit 2: The Fine and Performing Arts

The following magazines explore the concerns and happenings of the world of fine art and performance.

American Art (profiles American artists)

American Artist (discusses artistic techniques and materials)

American Theater (covers playwrights, actors and actresses, and directors across the country)

Dance Magazine (for and about dancers)

Popular Photography (for anyone who enjoys photography)

Rolling Stone (highlights rock and popular music)

Look for these books to find out more about African American artists:

Bearden, Romare and Henderson, Harry. *A History of African American Artists: From 1792 to the Present.* New York: Pantheon, 1993.

Bearden, Romare and Henderson, Harry. *Six Black Masters of American Art.* New York: Zenith Books, 1972.

Unit 3: The Sciences and Mathematics

To learn more about science, watch for "Nova" specials on public television. These programs discuss scientific breakthroughs, and interview scientists. You might also enjoy the following magazines:

Byte (for and about computer programmers)

Discover (news of science)

The Futurist (theories of the future)

PC Computing (for users of personal computers)

Popular Science (the mechanics of scientific instruments)

Prevention (news about health)

Scientific American (covers health, ecology, space, and more)

Read about the first African American in space:

Haskins, James. *Space Challenger: The Story of Guion Bluford.* Minneapolis: Carolrhoda, 1984.

Find out more about careers in engineering through:

National Council for Minorities in Engineering (NACME), c/o Aileen Walter, 3 W. 35th Street, New York, NY 10001; 212/279-2626, extension 213.

You can contact NASA for more information about the U.S. space program:

National Aeronautics and Space Administration, Lyndon B. Johnson Space Center, Houston, TX 77058.

Unit 4: Business and Public Service

For up-to-date news on government, politics, education, and economics around the world, look for the magazines *Newsweek, Time,* and *U.S. News and World Report.* You might also enjoy the following business publications:

Business Week (a magazine about business)

Ebony (topics of special interest to African Americans)

Forbes (top U.S. businesses and the people who run them)

Money (a magazine for and about business people)

Learn more about John Johnson in his autobiography:

Johnson, John H. *Succeeding Against the Odds.* New York: Warner, 1989.

You can also contact these agencies for more information on African American rights and history:

The National Association for the Advancement of Colored People (NAACP), 4805 Mt. Hope Drive, Baltimore, MD 21215-3297.

Schomburg Center for Research in Black Culture, 515 Lenox Avenue, New York, NY 10031.

INDEX